# BEAT THAT PARKING TICKET

# Beat That Parking Ticket

## A Complete Guide for New York City

Haskell Nussbaum

Gavel Press
New York

Published by Gavel Press, POB 20432, New York, NY, 10001-0008, USA
www.gavelpress.com

This book is available at quantity discounts for bulk purchases. For orders or further information contact info@gavelpress.com.
This publication is designed to provide information with regard to the subject matter covered solely for educational purposes. While all the stories and anecdotes described in the book are based on true experiences, some situations and letters have been changed slightly. It is sold with the understanding that it is not meant to be legal or professional advice and if such advice or other expert assistance is required, the services of a competent professional person should be sought. The Author and Publisher specifically disclaim any liability, loss, or risk which is incurred as a consequence, directly or indirectly, of the use and application of any of the contents of this work.

Cover art by George Foster
Typeset by Jerusalem Typesetting

ISBN 10: 0-9786825-6-4
ISBN 13: 978-0-9786825-6-9

Publisher's CIP Data
Nussbaum, Haskell.
Beat that parking ticket: a complete guide for new york city / by Haskell Nussbaum.
 p cm.
Includes index.
ISBN 10: 0-9786825-6-4
ISBN 13: 978-0-9786825-6-9
1. New York (NY) – Guidebooks. 2. Automobile parking – Law and legislation – New York (State) – New York. 3. Traffic regulations – New York (State) – New York. I. Title
F128.18 2006
917.47'1 dc22 Library of Congress Control Number: 2006908154

Printed in the United States of America.

10 9 8 7 6 5 4 3 2 1

Visit this book's website at www.BeatThatParkingTicket.com

To the Judge:

I recently visited New York and was given this parking ticket. I would sooner pay Osama bin Laden than pay this ticket. I don't know why any sane person would drive a car in New York City anyway. Nor why anyone would live there when there are so many open and greener places to live where the costs of living are lower.

And, by the way, here parking tickets are only $5.

*Letter received by New York City's Parking Bureau*

*To my parents,*
*for being such wonderful role models.*

# Contents

# Introduction

I've been a corporate lawyer, a judicial clerk for a judge on the Supreme Court of Israel, a freelance writer, a soldier and even (briefly) a day trader. But no day job I've ever held has generated as much interest among strangers and friends alike as the one where they used to call me "judge."

I worked in the City of New York's Parking Bureau for only six months or so, but during that time I adjudicated thousands of parking tickets, argued with (and learned from) many senior judges, and kept a running record of the funniest and strangest cases that I and my fellow judges came across.

I also kept bumping into people who wanted to know how the system "really" worked. The question was always the same: What was the *best* way for them to fight their ticket(s)?

The result is this book.

This is the most comprehensive – and entertaining – book about parking tickets that you'll ever find. It contains information that is simply impossible to obtain if you haven't actually worked as a parking ticket judge. Whether you live in New York, Chicago, Los Angeles,

Toronto, London, Melbourne or Tokyo, you have fire hydrants, handicapped zones and signs telling you where not to park. And although each city has its own way of settling tickets (and this book will concentrate on New York), what they all have in common is that every city has judges who decide whether to believe your case. And now, finally, you have a guide that will allow you to get into the head of the judge deciding on your ticket.

Every day, judges see and hear the same excuses from people looking to get out of their tickets. And every day many of those pleas get pushed aside with about the same level of attention as you would devote to plucking off a stray hair that falls on your jacket. If for no other reason than that, you need to read this book. It's simply too frustrating to spend hours waiting to see a judge, with all the headaches that come with that, only to give him an excuse that never had any chance of flying.

And this is doubly true if you actually had a valid defense that would have worked – if only you knew about it. In fact, you might be surprised at all the defenses that could work for you. There are defenses based on the law which many people – including many traffic cops – simply get wrong. Or aren't aware of. There are technical defects that are not obvious or well known, but are well worth searching for. And there are tickets that are perfectly valid but are *still* worth fighting, if only for the possibility of a reduction in the fine. For all of these tickets, knowledge of what has – and hasn't – worked in the past is real power.

In New York City, over ten million parking tickets are issued every single year. Fines have been going up and cops have been getting quicker at their game. The result has been that millions of tickets are getting adjudicated by the Parking Bureau's judges – often at a lightning rate. Your defense, whether you go to a live hearing or submit it by mail or internet, has approximately one minute to sway the judge (the other few minutes are taken up by the judge writing out the verdict in the format prescribed by the Bureau). Make that minute count. Read this book thoroughly and take note of any defenses that could apply to you. Listen to my advice about *how* to defend your ticket; there are times when mailing in your defense will suit you best and times when you must go to a live hearing to have a chance of winning. Perk your ears up when I mention an obscure law or rule that could mean the difference between being found guilty or innocent.

And, finally, enjoy the read. I've tried to include not just information but amusing stories too. Excuses that were simply wild and letters so outrageous that they are not to be believed. This is, after all, New York. And in New York, even fighting a parking ticket can be fun.

# PART I

## GENERAL DEFENSES:
*Defenses that can potentially work on almost any violation*

# 1. Technical Defects – the Easiest Way to Beat a Ticket

There's nothing quite like getting off a ticket because of a technical defect. It's so sweet: You parked illegally, you got caught and they've got you dead to rights. And then, suddenly, you notice the defect – and the sun shines brighter as the gods grin at your narrow escape. A leprechaun caressing his pot of gold could not find a better fortune – for a defective ticket is found money.

But how often, you might wonder, are the tickets defective?

More often than you may think. I don't have any official statistics to back me up, but both in my own experience and in the experience of the judges I queried, the number of tickets that get dismissed "not on the merits" of the case because the cop made a technical mistake is probably between 10% and 25% of all the tickets that are fought.

Let's think about that for a moment. New York City issues around ten million parking tickets each year, and only about two million of them are actively fought.

3

Simple math suggests that of the eight million tickets that are just paid up without a peep, there are probably *at least* 800,000 tickets that are defective. Even if you want to be really conservative and say that the reason people are just paying is that they've checked and haven't seen any defects, it stands to reason that at least one in ten people will miss something – most likely because they didn't really know what to look for. That's a solid 80,000 tickets that could be thrown out, with the money staying in your pockets, rather than traveling to city coffers.

If I convince you of nothing else in this book, then let it be this: it is always worth fighting your ticket and asking that it be reviewed for technical defects.

So, now that I've convinced you (I hope) to look for technical defects, how do you spot one?

First off, you don't really have to.

By now you may be saying to yourself: Huh? I thought it always paid to check. And it does. But the good news is that all of the judges are trained to always review every ticket for technical defects and to dismiss those tickets that have any. What's more, and this ain't obvious, judges have a kind of incentive to find a defect – because we can get through so many more tickets in any given day if we only have to spend twenty seconds on a ticket that's easily thrown out. And while there is no quota on how many tickets we have to judge per day, it always looks better to be more "productive."

> You will find that the state is the kind of organization which, though it does big things badly, does small things badly, too.
>
> – John Kenneth Galbraith

So, if the judges will check anyway, is there any point in going into details?

The short answer is: yes. Because judges are human. And there will be some judges who check more carefully than others. And some judges will be too lazy to check at all. But if you know enough to direct our attention to the problem – you not only make our lives easier, you also make it more likely that we don't inadvertently miss something.

So, what are we looking for? Just what *is* a technical defect anyway, and how do you spot one?

Simply put, a defective ticket is one that is either missing something or is inaccurate about something – as long as that "something" is crucial to the ticket being considered valid. Which isn't actually as simple as all that.

Let's walk through this.

Just what does a ticket need in order to be valid?

## Legibility
Well, first of all, it needs to be legible.

You might think that this would be obvious, or straightforward, but in fact, it isn't. Some of the stickiest fights between ticket-fighters ("respondents", as judges call 'em) and judges revolve around the legibility, or lack thereof, of the ticket.

Many is the time that a respondent will claim that the ticket is illegible – and to the "untrained" eyes of a normal human being it isn't. But to the eyes of a judge used to routinely deciphering the hieroglyphics of a parking cop's scrawl, the ticket is as clear as the Rosetta Stone. We're simply too used to seeing the shorthand that cops have developed in the course of writing tickets by hand all day every day. What to you looks like scribble, to us looks like "overtime parking in a missing meter zone."

In defense of outraged respondents, though, one of my pet peeves with the Parking Bureau is just how many tickets that are not really legible are adjudicated and convicted anyway. What happens often is this: the ticket that comes up on the screen in front of the judge – the official ticket – is ambiguous. But just slightly. If all we had to go by would be that screen, it wouldn't be obvious that the letter on the plate is a "K" rather than an "R" (for example). But the ticket-fighter helpfully provided his or her own copy of the ticket. And *that* copy is clear (or clearer, at any rate), which helps the judge "see" the proper letter on the screen. And voilà, the ticket is deemed "legible."

> Your Honor:
>
> I only had dollar bills on me that day and the meter only takes coins. By denying me the ability to pay using paper bills the government was violating its own rules that a dollar bill is "legal tender for all debts, public and private." To preserve our whole economy and system of paper currency, this ticket must be dismissed!

Technically, judges are not really allowed to use your copy – it's only the official copy on the screen that counts. But (and I think I've said this before), judges are human. We don't just "forget" the ticket now that we've seen it. Having read your copy properly, the copy on the screen is no longer ambiguous. What's more, there is a certain unspoken pressure (especially on newer judges still getting their decisions reviewed by senior judges) not to dismiss too many tickets due to legibility. This pressure got so bad in my "class" of new judges that one of my fellow trainees told me that he would find illegible tickets guilty despite the fact that they should have been dismissed, and would then mark them surreptitiously to see if the senior judge reviewing his work would catch on. Depressingly (especially for those whose tickets he adjudicated), he told me that the seniors never once called him on any of those summonses. That is, they all stayed guilty.

So, what's to be done? Notwithstanding the silliness of it all, your best move here is to simply *not* send or bring in your own copy of the ticket. Without your copy, the official ticket is the only one available for the judge to rely on and you have a fairly good chance that the imperfect technology the Parking Bureau uses to scan tickets into their system will work in your favor – and result in the dismissal of what otherwise would be a perfectly valid ticket.

Incidentally, I ought to point out that by the same logic (that judges will rely on the official ticket, at least officially), it never pays to try to "fix" your ticket to make it more illegible or ambiguous. Many is the time that we've seen people try to change the "N" of their license plates to an "M" on their copy of the ticket – an alteration that leaps off the screen at us, screaming "fraud!"

Which brings us to the next element that any self-respecting summons requires: a valid license plate.

## License Plate

For a ticket to be valid, it needs to state your license plate. And the plate needs to be correct.

> To the Judge:
> I'm on welfare so I shouldn't have to pay for this. The City giving me a ticket is defeating the state and federal governments' policy of trying to help me survive. In fact, the ticket is probably unconstitutional.

The license plate is your car's primary identifier. Everything in the system – whether it's the Parking Bureau's computers or the DMV – relies on your plate. It only stands to reason (besides the legal necessity of it) that if your plate is written incorrectly, the ticket is defective.

Most of the time, if the ticket is really off – the wrong plate entirely – you won't have to worry about it, because the notice will probably get sent to some other poor schmo, who will then have to fight a ticket he never should have received. (If you want to do the right thing, send in the ticket with an explanation, and save some nameless unfortunate the trouble of fighting City Hall.)

If the plate is merely illegible on your ticket – well you've read the section above about legibility (or you should have). Follow my advice – and pray for the best.

Incidentally, the best case I ever saw of someone cleverly working the system vis-à-vis license plates was the guy who bought himself vanity plates with something like "T0P1OO" – spelled counter-intuitively, with a zero between the "T" and "P" and using the letter "O" *instead* of zeros, after the number 1. This plate had the potential to confuse both parking and traffic cops in a myriad of ways – and it did! It worked to get him off at least half a dozen tickets (gold star for ingenuity).

## The Location

If the location on the ticket is just dead wrong – the wrong number address or even the wrong street – then say hello to beating your ticket. Similarly, if the cop forgot to indicate whether your vehicle was in front of that address or on the opposite side of the street (resulting in an ambiguity) – then, too, the ticket will be quashed.

In fact, for most tickets the location that the cop writes on the ticket must be completely unambiguous. If the cop gets lazy (or doesn't know better) and fills in a description such as "c/o 169$^{th}$ + Bdwy" (i.e. corner of 169$^{th}$ St and Broadway), the ticket will be defective – because there are four corners to that intersection and on each corner there are two places (vertical and horizontal) that the car could be parked. For a violation that depends on a specific sign, such ambiguity kills the ticket dead.

But there *are* some exceptions to the unambiguous location rule – and those are status or equipment violations. If they nab you for one of these violations (for example, a missing inspection sticker) then they don't have to be as clear about the location. The theory behind this is that you're not supposed to have this vehicle on *any* public roadway – so we're less concerned that we don't know exactly which corner the car was parked on.

## The Color and/or Year of the Vehicle

We get many excited respondents who gleefully point to these sections on their tickets and proclaim, often in a loud voice, "the color's wrong! My car is tan – not brown!"

I'm sorry to have to do it, but I'm bursting this bubble. Unfortunately, the law does *not* require these elements to be on the ticket at all. As a result, the Parking Bureau considers them "immaterial" and "irrelevant." The only exceptions are where you can point to these sections to help you prove that the registration (for example) is completely wrong – i.e. the ticket isn't really yours. In such a case, the fact that the color and the year are *also* wrong help strengthen your case that the ticket was issued to the wrong license plate to begin with.

## Type of License Plate

For most of us, traveling in regular "passenger" vehicles, the type of license plate is simple for the ticketing cop to get right, so it's relatively rare to be able to get out of a ticket due to him writing down the wrong type. Still, it is possible – and this is one that you should definitely check out if you have vanity plates, since vanity plates have their own "type." If your vanity plates look "un-vanity like," then you may get away with all kinds of tickets. For example, a vanity plate with a few random letters and numbers, assuming the DMV allows you to have it, could conceivably fool a traffic cop into thinking that it was a regular "passenger" license plate – and cause him to write down the wrong type.

This is generally a better defense for commercial vehicles – because officers can easily check off the wrong type out of habit. For example, an "apportioned" license plate (given to trucks and the like who are registered in the International Registration Program (IRP) of commercial carriers), must be labeled

A Partial List of Plate Types:

PAS – Passenger or suburban cars

COM – Commercial

IRP – International Registration Plan

SRF – Special Passenger

DLR – Dealer

NYS – New York Senate

MED – Medical Doctor

OML – Omnibus, Livery

AMB – Ambulance

SNO – Snowmobiles

SPO – Sports

"APP" or "IRP" – not "com." Sloppy cops, however, may tick off the "com" box out of habit. And here I'll quote a senior judge who opined to me that "cops are very careless. It's not to be believed the number of errors that cops make."

To which I say "amen" and "thank you" on behalf of irate car owners everywhere, now smiling because they got off of an otherwise valid ticket.

## Registration

Here's an easy one: the registration expiration date must be complete on the ticket. Otherwise, you guessed it: it's a defective ticket.

For NY-registered vehicles, this means that the officer had better fill in the exact date of the registration expiration date – including the day; not just the month and year. (For out-of-state vehicles ticketed in New York whatever appears on the plate suffices.)

Also, and this isn't so obvious, if your registration sticker is missing or mutilated and the cop can't read it, he can't just write "not shown" in those boxes, or cross a line through them; he must also write down, on the ticket itself, the *reason* he couldn't write it – the reason it wasn't shown (for example, that it had been "mutilated"). If he forgets (or his handwriting is completely illegible), you've just beaten a ticket. Of course, you'll probably get another one (so sad) – this time for "missing registration sticker."

## Body Type

Here is one that seems ridiculous to me, but it's on the books: the officer must get the body type of your vehicle correct. Generally, they get this off of your registration sticker (they should get *everything* off the sticker, legally) and if the info isn't there (for example, you have a temporary registration sticker) then they just have to provide a reasonable description of the body type.

Where this gets fun is when cops get lazy (this is getting to be a common theme, isn't it?) and use their "common sense" instead of the sticker. In one memorable case that I had, a woman had five tickets – for crosswalk, pedestrian ramp, registration, inspection, and plates not matching, totaling hundreds of dollars (plus extra fines for being late) – all dismissed, because the cop claimed that her vehicle was a "sedan" instead of a "suburban." How's that for being one lucky lady?

## Out-of-State Vehicles

This isn't really a separate element of a ticket, and all of the technical defects above apply to out-of-state vehicles too, of course. But if you happen to get a ticket while visiting New York in your out-of-state car (or if you just never changed your car's registration, however wrong that may be), you should know a couple of things.

First, cops are more likely to get your plate type wrong. Lucky you. But second, and more importantly, you should be checking the registration part of your ticket carefully. There are plenty of officers who will simply write "N/S" ("not shown") for registration if the vehicle is from out-of-state, because it's the easy way to go. But if you *do* have a registration expiration date clearly marked on your plate, then send in a photograph. As long as the judge doesn't believe that you stuck it on post-factum you ought to be able to get the ticket dismissed. This is a trick that most out-of-state people don't know about.

On the other hand, you are at one disadvantage: when it comes to body types, the officers are allowed to get it wrong. All they have to do is fill in a "reasonable" approximation of the body type for the ticket to be valid.

## Other Defects

There are plenty of other things cops can get wrong, some of them obvious, some less so. For instance, if the officer writes on the ticket that the "no parking" sign is valid "anytime" but then checks off that the sign's hours are 7 AM to 7 PM, clearly that points to a defective ticket because the ticket is saying two contradictory things.

Or, for example, if the officer ticks off more than one violation on any given ticket – that's a no-no, since each ticket must only state one violation. Once again, you have a defective ticket.

A nice one is if the cop forgets the time altogether (AM? PM? Who knows?) Or forgets the license plate or registration (or really almost anything, other than color and year). But hey, there's no need to go into major detail over the obvious, right?

So let's end this section with a few things that may *not* be obvious.

First, electronic tickets. They're the way of the future and have far fewer defects, but even they should be scrutinized to find your get-out-of-this-fine-free card. For instance, I once saw an electronic ticket that claimed a car was parked overtime at a broken meter – but the cop had inadvertently left the ticket with the answer "yes" to the question "meter operational?" Clearly, if the meter was operational then it wasn't a "broken meter." Voilà, the makings of a defective ticket.

Second, here's something to think about: sometimes cops commit outright fraud. They hand you the ticket but forget to fill in one of the required elements. Or they got the time really wrong. When they look through their ticket-books later, they spot the problem and "fix it" themselves. The result? An official ticket that looks fine (although sometimes it clearly looks doctored) even though it wasn't kosher at all. In this case, where the ticket is clearly omitting something and you have the original ticket in front of you – bring it in (or mail it). An obvious omission on the face of the ticket is probably the only exception to my advice given above to never mail in your copy of the ticket.

And while we're on the subject of cops, let's not forget something: they're not always the evil wolf. On occasion I've seen tickets where it was clear that the cop deliberately made the ticket defective, to be nice. The most blatant example I came across was one where an older lady parked her car illegally in order to go to church, and then actually spoke to the ticketing officer – who showed her how he left the box blank, so that she wouldn't have to pay it. Something she explained to me in great detail.

Finally, there are two more little-known ways of fighting on a technicality and winning. The first one is to protest the lack of personal service, where it applies. And the second goes to the issue of the ticketing officer's identity. Let's look at these a bit more closely.

Under the law, if the cop sees the person "operating" the vehicle, he or she must serve that person individually – not just by putting the ticket under the wipers. There's a fair amount of confusion on this point even among people who know about it, so let me clear this up: according to the Parking Bureau, a person is only "operating" a vehicle if he or she is behind the wheel. *Not* if he's running down the block trying to stop the cop from giving him a ticket. And yes, that person behind the wheel must be awake.

This used to be a better defense – until parking tickets.com started using it almost pro-forma. It's far more difficult nowadays to convince a judge that you really were behind the wheel, saw the officer, and that the officer didn't give you the ticket personally. Still, if it happened that way – you do have a good defense. This is probably one of the times that you should fight the ticket in person, so that you can be as persuasive as possible that you really did speak to or see the cop and that he ignored you.

And then there's the question of the cop's identity.

When I first started working as a parking ticket judge there was a debate regarding the Parking Bureau's policy on this issue. The trouble was that under the law, the cop's signature did not need to be legible for the ticket to be valid (it did, however, need to be there; if it's missing outright, the ticket is defective). But in practice, the cop's name and/or badge number was often illegible too. Or missing altogether (often due to bad scanning of the ticket into the system, I suspect, since the badge number is stamped onto the ticket in faint ink, especially late in the day, which is difficult for the scanners to pick up). The result was that these tickets had no identifiable officer. Just who *was* that masked man giving out tickets?

So they changed the policy, and suddenly, if the badge number was missing on the official ticket – the ticket went out the window too. Before you knew it, there were so many defective tickets that the senior judges started getting antsy. All those tickets getting dismissed!

So they changed the policy again. And now it's okay if the number is gone, as long as there is *some* way of identifying the officer. Any way will do. If his name is legible – OK. If his name is a scrawl, but we can see the badge number – no problem (incidentally, the precinct number is not a required element of the ticket, in case you were thinking that that's a way out). Needless to say, the number of defective tickets suddenly plummeted.

So, the upshot is this: if the officer's name and signature are completely illegible *and* if the number is either gone or is very faint – it pays to bring it to a judge's attention. And, of course, do *not* bring in or mail in your copy of the ticket – for if there *is* a scanning problem (and the faint ink on your copy is now gone in the scanned copy), there's no need for you to tempt the judge to "fix it" in his head.

> *The Authority for Dismissing a Ticket Based on a Missing Signature:* VTL Section 237(a) says that notice (i.e. a ticket) must be filled out *and* sworn to or affirmed by the officer. No signature – no "sworn to" or "affirmed by." And then hop on over to Section 238: if the notice is missing a required element, then, upon application [the ticket] shall be dismissed.

## Recap: The Least You Need to Know:

- It always pays to ask the judge to check the ticket for defects.
- It's almost never a good idea to bring in, or mail in,

your original copy of the summons, unless an element is clearly missing from it (just send in the summons number).

- The color and year are not necessary for the ticket
  to be valid.
- Always check the plate number, registration, body
  type, plate type, make or model of the vehicle, and
  the time and location that are stated on the face of
  the ticket.
- Check the ticket's legibility – the most common reason for dismissal.
- Read Part II of this book to check out hidden technical defects that can occur for specific violations.

# 2. My Car Broke Down

It happens, at one point or another, to almost everyone: our cars break down. They blow tires, leak gas, start smoking under the hood, or do some other unforeseeable action to themselves and stop working, right in the middle of us driving them. Or perhaps they seemed just fine the night before, when we parked them, but now they simply refuse to start. Either way, there we are, with a vehicle that won't do what we tell it to – and a ticket under our wipers, because some dumb traffic cop refused to listen to reason.

It seems so unfair when this happens – doubly unfair, truthfully, because everyone knows that if the car was running properly, it wouldn't be parked there – and that on top of the ticket, the towing bill alone is going to cost a fortune.

But take heart. If you are unfortunate enough to have been ticketed while "disabled" you are, at least, lucky enough that you have a good defense, as long as you use it properly. And using the "disabled vehicle" defense properly is what this section is all about. Because although it seems like it ought to be simple, it's rather amazing how easy it is to screw this one up.

## How to use this defense:

To start with, you have to know that it isn't enough to just say that the car was disabled. Many people don't know this, but it's a law that you must expeditiously remove your disabled vehicle(s) from the street. So right off the bat you should know that to get your parking ticket dismissed you're going to have to prove three things:

(1) Your vehicle was disabled;

(2) It was pushed to the side of the road; and

(3) It was removed, as soon as humanly possible.

I can't stress enough that this is one of those defenses where it helps to have proof. For example – a towing bill.

Please, I beg you, don't try to be "clever," and figure that we'll never know the difference. For instance, there was one lady who claimed that her car broke down in the middle of the crosswalk, and that while she was calling in the tow truck from a payphone down the street, she received a ticket. This, by itself, was not unbelievable. But the woman in question hadn't submitted any towing bill (or anything else to support her claim) and, to make matters more suspicious, I noticed at least two more tickets, given on two dates, that she was fighting using the very same defense. With my curiosity piqued, I searched her record for other tickets. And there they were. I found no less than seven other letters from her, fighting all types of parking violations, all using the same defense. And none with any towing bills. This was in my first month of the job, and I soon learned a simple rule: If there is no documentation, it's hard to believe that the car was really towed.

So – submit your bill. But don't just leave it at that. The bill may say that the car was broken and removed from the street, but unless the tow truck driver put in an exact time on the invoice, it still doesn't satisfy the needs of the "disabled vehicle" defense. For the removal must be "expeditious."

It's downright silly to have a great defense and then mess it up because you left out something as easy to fill in as that. So, before you send in the bill – check to see if it's properly dated and the time is there. If it isn't, don't fret – just be sure to tell us (preferably when you come down in person, if you want us to believe you) what time the tow truck arrived. And, yes, of course you will have more credibility regarding this, if you're actually there when the tow truck comes.

> Is fuel efficiency really what we need most desperately? I say what we really need is a car that can be shot when it breaks down.
>
> – Russell Baker

And while you're at it, tell us what the problem with the car was. Don't assume that we will be able to figure out some garage mechanic's scrawl, just because you can. The rule of thumb here is simple: the easier you make life for the judge, the less likely it is that something will go wrong.

Also, the car needs to really and truly be *disabled*. Not just out of gas or with the keys locked inside. There has to be something actually wrong with it. And you can't have parked illegally and only then become "disabled." It's a downright silly defense, if you think about it, to claim that you were illegally double-parked but then couldn't avoid the parking cop coming to ticket you because your car wouldn't start. Don't be a dope.

Make sure that your defense doesn't crumble when the judge asks "when did the car become disabled?"

Finally, there's one real caveat to the disabled vehicle defense: it doesn't usually work if you're at a hydrant. It isn't particularly obvious that any normal driver would know this, but unless you are somehow legally parked by the hydrant to begin with, even an expeditious removal of your broken car won't help you get a hydrant ticket dismissed. Or, as one senior judge once explained it to me, "the City would prefer you to even double park than to block a hydrant." The moral of the story? Don't push your broken car to the open spot before checking for hydrants.

### Recap: The Least You Need To Know:
- To use a disabled vehicle defense, you must show three things:
(1) The car was truly disabled;
(2) It was pushed to the side of the road; and
(3) It was expeditiously removed.
- Do NOT push your car to a space near a fire hydrant.

## 3. The Rules Were Not In Effect

Whenever I was having a slow day – say I had only judged ten or twelve mailed-in tickets by noon – I would pray that I would wade into a stack of tickets claiming that the rules were not in effect on the day the ticket was given. Why? Because they were so easy. After all, what's to argue about? Nine times out of ten all the judge needs to do is to check the date on the ticket, compare it to the mental calendar in his head and toss out the charges while wondering why the cops bothered to write them.

But then there's that one time in ten. The one where the impoverished student wails that she got a ticket for "no standing" on Martin Luther King Jr. Day – and isn't that a holiday? To make matters worse, the student (probably an Ivy Leaguer) knew that the cops had "screwed up" – and decided to wait until $60 worth of late penalties had piled up – smug in the knowledge that the ticket would be thrown out.

Oops. Better check the fine print, Miss. Martin Luther King Jr. Day is not a "major legal holiday." Which means all those "no standing" rules are marching on, fully in effect.

Actually, it's rather amazing how many people make this mistake. And every time I had to write "guilty" as their verdict, I felt lousy. It was such an honest mistake, after all. And if the charge was for "no standing" I couldn't even reduce the damages – which was often a ticket of at least $115 plus late fees.

So what *are* the rules about holidays? When can you plead that the rules were not in effect, and be allowed to be smug?

> **Learn from the mistakes of others – you can never live long enough to make them all yourself.**
>
> **– John Luther**

Basically, only in two consistent cases: (1) when the rules really were suspended; and (2) when the sign governing the space that you parked in was (for whatever reason) not in effect.

Let's take a look at this a bit closer.

## When The Rules Are Suspended:

If the rules really were suspended on the day that you got your ticket then you get a free pass. But double check before you park that you know just which rules are suspended. In New York, for instance, all parking rules, including "no stopping," "no standing" and "no parking" signs, are suspended on "major legal holidays" unless the sign is a 7-days-a-week sign. In other words, if the sign is generally valid "any time" or for specific hours on every day of the week, then it is still valid on Christmas. Otherwise – it's suspended.

But this obviously begs the question (as our impoverished student from above might ask): just what is a "major" legal holiday? Isn't Martin Luther King Jr. Day pretty major – especially in New York? What about Yom Kippur? Or Easter? God knows that those last two days are pretty important – downright "major," even – to Jews and Christians, respectively.

But the answer resides (rather dryly, I'm afraid) in black letter law. And the answer is, courtesy of Section 4–08 of the Traffic Rules found in Title 34, Chapter 4 of the Official Compilation of the Rules of the City of New York, that only Christmas, New Year's, Memorial Day, Independence Day, Labor Day, and Thanksgiving are "major" enough to suspend all those parking rules.

Feeling dissed? I mean, what about Rosh Hashanah, Holy Thursday, Good Friday, Passover, Id-ul-Adha – or even Martin Luther King Jr. Day? Any prizes for these "second-class" holidays?

Actually, yes. As you probably already know if you've ever parked in the Big Apple, all these holidays have *some* rules suspended too. Just not as many as the "major" holidays have.

Here are the rules for the non-major holidays:

## When Alternate-Side Parking is Suspended:

For all the "non-major" holidays (I'll list them below) only "alternate side parking" rules are suspended. Primarily, this means street-cleaning rules. Essentially, what the city is saying to its residents is that on certain festive days of the year the City gets to celebrate too – by staying dirty. (Anyone with a small child will no doubt appreciate the logic here).

Besides the street-cleaning rules (look for the signs with the picture of a broom on them), signs that restrict parking for only one or two ("alternate") days per week, and for at least six hours, are also suspended on all the "minor" holidays.

Got that? I hope so. Because plenty of the cops giving out tickets probably don't care to look at all the fine print. They're too busy giving out tickets. And I'd bet dollars to doughnuts that most cops wouldn't know, if asked, when half of these "minor" holidays occur.

For the record, there are plenty of them. New York lists all of these holidays as being worthy of alternate-side-parking rules being suspended: Yom Kippur, Rosh Hashanah, Holy Thursday, Good Friday, Ascension Thursday, Feast of the Assumption, Feast of All Saints, Feast of the Immaculate Conception, the first two days of Succoth, Shemini Atzereth, Simchas Torah, Shavuot, Orthodox Holy Thursday, Orthodox Good Friday, the first two and last two days of Passover, Id-ul-Fitr, Id-ul-Adha, all state and national holidays, Martin Luther King Jr.'s birthday, Lincoln's birthday, Washington's birthday, Columbus Day, Election Day, Veterans' Day – and any other day that the Commissioner announces.

Which leaves me with only one question: why not Valentine's Day? Does the City have no heart? Hell, I'm even willing to call it by its original "Saint Valentine" if it means not having to move the car...

### Non-Holidays When Alternate-Side Parking is Suspended:

Besides holidays (major and minor) there are always at least a few days that the City announces that alternate side parking rules are suspended. Usually, these are days that the city is snowed in. Or snowed under (sounds more dramatic that way, doesn't it? Although as someone who grew up in a city with major blizzards(up in the Great White North of Canada), I'm always amused at some New Yorkers' reactions to a mere foot of the white stuff).

On days like that, what you need to know is that it's not always good enough to just tell the judge that the radio announced that alternate side parking was suspended that day.

Sure, the Parking Bureau theoretically keeps track of all these days, and marks them on the calendars that the judges have before them. But what if the Bureau screwed up? Or, worse, what if the radio show that you relied on got it wrong?

This very case crossed my desk on my first week on the job. A man who was fighting his ticket via the internet claimed that his favorite radio show had announced that alternate side parking rules were suspended due to snow. So how dare those cops, he bellowed, write him a ticket?

Easily, I thought. Because a very thorough check of the calendar revealed no such snow day. Since the ticket-fighter had responded by internet, he didn't include any real proof that the radio show had actually made the announcement. Yes, he generously provided the name of the show and the station it was broadcast on – but what was I going to do with that? Call the station and wait until I tracked down a transcript of the show – which someone there would read to me? Not only did I have no time (or patience) for that – I didn't even have access to a phone.

So I did what I thought was most fair – I adjourned the ticket to give him the chance to hunt down a written transcript and send it in as proof. And then watched as the senior judge reviewing my work reprimanded me for being naïve and instructed me to "re-think" the case – very unsubtle code telling me to find him guilty.

The lesson? Always bring proof. If you relied on a radio announcement, obtain a transcript; if a newspaper published it, include a clipping. Even better, schlep the silly reporter down to the judge with you and let *him* testify (you'll get points for creativity, if nothing else).

> Defense: I tried telling the officer that I had every right to park there. But he refused to listen to me as he shouted "yeah, yeah, that's what they all say." He was very arrogant.
>
> Where I come from that just wouldn't happen.
>
> Don't your mothers teach you better manners?

All of which is to say that if you want to fight a ticket based on rules not being in effect – know your holidays or bring proof of any exceptions (and see my two caveats later in the section).

## The Sign Wasn't In Effect

The second variation of the "rules not in effect" defense is that the particular sign that you violated wasn't in effect at the time that you got the ticket.

This is a great – and easy – defense to claim. Bear in mind, though, that it's a different claim than the defense of the sign being missing, damaged or illegible; for those defenses, see Chapter 9.

There are really only two cases that fall under this rubric. The first case is where the cop got the time wrong, and the violation either hadn't started yet or had already ended. The second case is when, due to snow or some other obstruction, the violation couldn't be avoided, because there was, effectively, no notice of it.

In the first case, the classic example is the car that gets ticketed for a street-cleaning violation and the time on the ticket shows the violation occurring only one or two minutes after the sign started. The driver's defense is that the cop jumped the gun. While we'll go into more detail on this in the separate violations section of this book, for now it's enough to know that if your defense is that the cop's watch was "fast," and the time is close, you'll probably win your claim. You have, essentially, made the claim that the sign's rule was not yet in effect.

The second case, where snow, for example, is blocking the hydrant or pedestrian ramp, relies more on your credibility. Your defense is that the violation was not in effect because it was impossible for you to have known the ramp was there (the legal terminology here is that you had no notice). For this defense to work, you generally need proof – particularly pictures. Take lots of them (cover the whole block) and point out when you see or write to the judge that the pedestrian ramp was impossible *not* to miss (and see the separate chapter about pedestrian ramps later). If this doesn't work – well, bear in mind that you can always appeal. Appeals, by the way, are a good reason to always keep copies of the pictures you send in.

Finally, I'll conclude this section on "rules not in effect" with one major and one minor caveat.

## The Major Caveat: Never Trust A Cop

The major caveat to the "rules were not in effect" defense is that whether you're claiming that all the rules were suspended or just those particular signs, the worst possible proof that you can bring up is to say that "I asked the traffic cop, and that's what he told me."

I can't stress this enough – because I can't count how many times we've all heard it – that this is not proof that the rules or signs were really not in effect.

Sometimes I used to wonder whether the traffic cops do this out of spite or conspiracy, but ultimately I concluded that it was either out of genuine ignorance or simply the desire to not have to deal with the driver(s) anymore.

The usual defense we hear runs like this: The first cop told you it was okay, you relied on him/her "in good faith" and then got ticketed by a different police officer, not five minutes later. Sound familiar? Sometimes this happens when the sign is just confusing, but it can also easily happen when a cop wants to accommodate you. Or just doesn't know.

For example, we would often get letters from churchgoers that claimed that the cops "knew" not to ticket their cars on those mornings that prayers were held. Yet somehow they got a ticket. Often, the person defending her ticket can even describe the officer who assured her that she could park there.

Unfortunately, none of that matters. The cop simply doesn't have the authority to "overrule" the legislated, written traffic rules except in very specific circumstances. And the last word on how to "interpret" any given sign is not a cop's. It's a parking judge's. And most judges are not, frankly, impressed by some anonymous traffic officer's legal analysis. So – save yourselves a guilty verdict, and don't rely on a cop's word alone.

Finally, one last caveat:

### The Minor Caveat: When ASP rules are suspended, meters still rule

It's easy to forget that not *all* rules are suspended on days that alternate side parking rules are. However, the trap that too many people fall into is forgetting that their vehicle, now safe from street cleaning prohibitions, is still subject to paying for any meters.

So if you're at a space where a meter applies – don't forget to pay it (and don't listen to any cops or passersby telling you differently, either).

Otherwise, the rules-not-in-effect defense is still, hands-down, one of the best.

## Recap: The Least You Need to Know

- There are two types of rules-not-in-effect defenses:
(1) The rules were suspended that day.
(2) The sign wasn't in effect.
- There are only six "major" legal holidays – Christmas, New Year's, Memorial Day, Independence Day, Labor Day and Thanksgiving.
- On "major" holidays all parking, standing and stopping rules are suspended except for those that are in effect seven days a week.
- On minor holidays, only ASP rules are suspended. Meters and other signs still apply.
- If your defense relies on snow or announcements in the press, always submit proof.
- If the cop's watch was "fast" or "slow" your defense is that the sign wasn't in effect.
- Never trust a cop's parking rules wisdom: they aren't the final word on how signs or laws are interpreted.

## 4. I Didn't Do It – General Denials

"It wasn't me; it was the one-armed bandit."

Anyone who's seen *The Fugitive* can sympathize with the innocent man wrongly convicted of a crime. But the purpose of this section is to help you sympathize with the *judge*. The hanging judge. Who strangely enough might actually deserve your sympathy.

They hear it all the time. It's the famous "I didn't do it" defense. And, in a word, it's lousy.

The problem with this defense – the general denial – is not that it may not be the truth, but that it's so difficult to prove. And proof is what every trial is about.

Oh, I know. As trials go, a parking ticket is hardly a blip on the screen. And if you send in your defense by mail or via the internet, it probably never occurs to you to think of the judge as weighing your words as "evidence."

Nevertheless, every time a parking ticket judge listens to your words or reads them on paper, he or she is listening to *testimony* – and is weighing its credibility against the officer's credibility (the one who wrote the ticket). And, generally, you will lose.

The trouble is that we all know that you have a great

incentive to lie. And as the fines on parking tickets rise, so does everyone's motivation to lie their way out of them.

This is so true that during training sessions for new judges, the senior judges teaching the codes that are entered into the computer system stress that the code for the defense "general denial" is almost inevitably followed by the code for "not credible."

This is so true that when my friend came to me one day, livid over a ticket that he had received even though his car was "nowhere near the meter," my only advice was to tell him to prepare to pay the ticket. I mean, *I* believed him; he's my friend. But who else would?

Still, if that's what happened to you and you have no choice but to use a general denial, then this section should at least teach you how to do it well.

> If I tell a lie it's only because I think I'm telling the truth.
>
> – Phil Gaglardi, Minister of Highways, British Columbia, Canada

To start with, don't be trite. I've heard many "I would never do something like that" defenses and not one of them sounded like anything other than a poor attempt to weasel out of a fine. After all, would you really "never" double park? If your child was sick? If you had to run in to the bathroom? If you were thinking that you'd only be there for two minutes?

And please, for heaven's sake, don't be ludicrous. Don't be like the person who claimed that he had parked in a specific spot, then moved his car, came back an hour later and found the exact same spot – just in time to get a ticket for overtime parking. Or the even crazier person who told a judge that his car had been stolen – and then returned, to the very same parking spot. The judge, a soft-spoken bloke, just blinked at him and with a straight face, asked him, "did the thief gas you up, too?"

Then there's my favorite category – those people who claim that their car was nowhere near that location, hell, their car was never even in the city – yet they enclose the original ticket with their defense. The ticket that can only be found *on the car*.

If you must use a general denial then the way to go is to stress that the police officer somehow made an error. We're all human, after all. And as one judge who had been in the Parking Bureau for well over ten years told me: "Cops are very careless. It's unbelievable how many mistakes cops make on these tickets."

If there's some reason to think that the cop really could be mistaken, don't be scared to include it. For instance, I had one ticket where the defense was that the driver of the car was himself an ex-cop who knew the law and who wouldn't have parked at a hydrant. To this he added that he had phoned the precinct where the ticketing officer worked and discovered that the officer who had ticketed his car had only recently begun working as a traffic officer. Naturally, I was inclined to believe him. So inclined, in fact, that I checked the records of other tickets that this officer wrote, to look for obvious signs of a beginner's errors. Which, in fact, I found.

The point here is that you have to help the judges help you. Provide some reason, preferably a good reason, that the officer got it wrong.

But one word of caution: don't, please, let your reason be simply that you've parked there before without getting a ticket. I had one lady who indignantly proclaimed that she had parked her convertible in "that very same spot" for the previous nine days without receiving a ticket – so obviously the cop was wrong. The only thing obvious to me was that this lady should have been kissing the asphalt under her convertible for having gotten ten days of illegal parking for the price of only one ticket.

Finally, you may be tempted to follow in the illustrious footsteps of so many other offenders by figuring that if you drove off while the cop was writing your ticket, you can simply deny that you were ever there. This has happened so often that the cops are almost always more believable than you. What they do, quite simply, is to write the words "drove off" on the top of the ticket. And every judge understands that the driver's denial is not persuasive. This is especially true when the offense is double parking and we know that you were in a position to make your getaway quickly.

On a last note about denials, however, there is one small ray of hope if you sent in a general denial and were found guilty. That hope is called an *appeal*.

> Whoever undertakes to set himself up as a judge of Truth and Knowledge is shipwrecked by the laughter of the gods.
>
> – Albert Einstein

Many judges are not careful about the way they word their verdicts when it comes to general denials. It's all too tempting to simply write "the respondent's claim fails to persuade me that the officer/ticket was incorrect" or some such similar statement. By including the words "officer" or "ticket" the judge has inadvertently told the absolute truth – that the ticket is more believable.

But, as one appeals judge said to me, "if the judge says that he didn't believe you because the officer said the opposite, it will get reversed – otherwise, why bother even having a judge?" It's a subtle difference that we're talking about. The judge should have said that the defense was not persuasive in its own right. The idea here is that when a judge listens to your testimony (or reads it) he is really presiding over a mini-trial. First came the officer's testimony (the ticket) and now comes yours. The judge doesn't have to think your testimony is credible – he can say that he's not persuaded by it. But if the only *reason* that he's unpersuaded is because the officer/ticket says the opposite – it sounds very much like the judge just didn't listen to your testimony at all. Which is a definite no-no. So, this is a subtle point, as I said. But in that subtle gap lies the hope of a dismissed ticket.

So, to sum up, use general denials only as a last re-sort and with great caution. And, if you do, I'll say to you simply this: good luck. You'll definitely need it.

**Recap: The Least You Need to Know**
- General denials are all about credibility – which ticket-fighters generally lack.
- Stress that the officer made a mistake and provide a good reason why.
- Having parked in that spot before is not a good rea-son.
- Driving off almost never works.
- If you lose, it's often worth appealing.

## 5. I Never Knew About the Ticket

I'm including this defense in this section not because it works, but just because it's so darn prevalent. Not a day goes by without at least a few hundred people making the case that they shouldn't have to pay for their ticket(s) simply because they never received them.

Actually, at first blush, this seems a fair argument – how can I be made to pay for something that I never knew about? But considering that after the ticket that you find on your car at least two notices are mailed to you, no judge is going to dismiss a ticket based on this defense.

So save your breath and don't even bother asking for a dismissal. But do ask the judge to waive at least the first late fee. After all, it's entirely reasonable that the ticket left under your wipers flew off and your first notice that you even had a ticket was the one mailed to you, that already included a late fee. Judges, who like to think of themselves as reasonable, will almost always reduce your ticket by at least the amount of the (first) late fee.

Of course, if you *are* claiming that you never received the ticket it ought to go without saying that you shouldn't write your claim on the back of the ticket itself (it's just amazing what you come across, as a judge). And please bear in mind that this defense might have some bearing on other statements you may be making in trying to get your tickets dismissed. For example, I always loved the chutzpah of the woman who wrote in saying that she had never received either the ticket or the notices – but that she had measured the distance from the hydrant *that day*. If she never got the ticket, how does she know? Of course, she probably meant that she just never parks too close to a hydrant; but where's her credibility for whatever happened *that* day?

Finally, if the reason that you never received some or all of the notices has to do with the fact that you recently moved make sure to mention this and include the exact dates of your move. You still won't get the ticket itself thrown out, but you stand a good chance of getting all the late fines abated, and even, if the ticket is already "in judgment" (see Chapter 27), getting it vacated down to the level where you can fight it on its merits.

> The road to truth is long, and lined the entire way with annoying bastards.
>
> – Alexander Jablokov

Oh, and one last thing. Don't bother getting all indignant about not getting the ticket. It doesn't help your case, it doesn't help your blood pressure, and it sure as hell doesn't impress the judge. Just mention it, ask for the fine to be reduced and move on to one of the other defenses available to fight the ticket on its merits. And good luck.

**Recap: The Least You Need to Know:**

- I never knew about the ticket is not a good defense.
- It will often work, however, in getting late fees reduced or waived.
- Do it gracefully, without yelling.

## 6. I Was Allowed to Park There – the Permit Defense

I love this defense. And if you've ever received a ticket for unauthorized parking when you have legitimate authorization, you have probably loved it too. After all, this is your get out of jail free card. Everyone *else* is toast – but *you* get to park there with impunity.

Now I know that you're probably none too happy with the numbskull cop who gave you the ticket (didn't he *see* the permit right there?), but here's where I suggest that you swallow that annoyance – and send us a copy of your permit.

I can't stress that enough: send us a copy. Please don't be lazy, like so many people, and just write in with your permit number. Nine times out of ten we won't know what kind of permit you really have, and to start investigating it on our own is too time-consuming to be efficient. If you don't send us a copy, you might, of course, get lucky and get the ticket dismissed or adjourned – but why take the chance? Believe me, there are plenty of "hanging judges" who will happily find you guilty, reasoning that you weren't being lazy at all, but sneaky, and didn't actually have the right permit.

Also, make sure that the permit you have matches the permit you needed for that spot. A Board of Education permit does not, for example, allow you to park near a hospital in a "Doctors Only" space, nor vice versa.

And while we're talking about Board of Education permits, teachers ought to know that technically, at least, the law requires that their permits identify the car that has the permit with a plate number and address. Although most judges will allow teachers' permits to be left blank, understanding that teachers don't want to mark their cars as targets for students to vandalize, from a legal standpoint that's just the Parking Bureau being nice.

And, by the way, if you are a teacher and you get ticketed for "No Parking – School Days," don't think that a permit frees you. "School Days" refers to a *time* that you are not allowed to park. Unless a sign explicitly allows cars with permits to park there on school days too – you'll be found guilty.

But what if you didn't yet have the permit, but were just about to get it? Can you still use the "authorized vehicle" defense?

Yes and no. If you already should have had the permit, but the authority issuing it has been dragging its feet, then you have a good case. For instance, City-issued permits for various housing projects are notorious for coming many months into the new year, despite the expiration

> Dear Judge,
>
> These parking tickets must stop. We can't cope with the unwarranted assault on our vehicles. Please show some courtesy and dismiss the ticket.
>
> Don't make me come down and fight it.

of the previous permits on December 31st. In this type of case, be sure to explicitly mention that the permit is deserved, and late through no fault of your own. And always include *proof* that the permit should be there. For example, a letter from the building's manager or from the principle of the school (in the case of a teacher's permit) will show that a permit is justified. Do *not* assume that the judge will connect the dots himself. Most judges spend less than five minutes on your case. Connect the dots for them.

If, however, your permit has not arrived because you've been late in applying for it, you're out of luck. Sure, we know that you're a teacher. You've included a letter from the principal, from parents, even from the school commissioner. But if you're a substitute teacher and you've never bothered applying for a permit before you got the ticket, you're just plumb out of a good excuse. Apply now, and avoid the next ticket.

Finally, if your permit is for doctors, for the press, or for being in handicapped zones – check out the chapters for those specific permits. And if you're authorized to park there because you're on "official business" (I got a Homeland Security permit once, and another time one that was marked with several letters that apparently meant undercover FBI) then you don't really need me to tell you that you'll get your ticket dismissed without too much hassle. Just try not to intimidate any of the more timid judges when you smile at them, and ask if "they feel lucky."

> I do not go outdoors. Not more than I have to. As far as I'm concerned, the whole point of living in New York City is indoors. You want greenery? Order the spinach.
>
> – David Rakoff

### Recap: The Least You Need to Know:

- Having a permit is a great defense.
- Always send in or bring in a copy of the permit.
- The permit must match the sign allowing that type of vehicle.
- If the permit is late in coming, explain why and provide proof that the lateness wasn't the product of your own fault.
- If you're a member of the press, an M.D., or have a permit to park in a handicapped zone, check out the specific chapters in this book dealing with those permits.

# 7. What – Again? Repeat Summonses

I was driving a foreign car, visiting New York (many years before becoming a parking ticket judge), and I parked in what I was certain was a perfectly legal spot before turning in for the night.

In the morning, there on my windshield, no less than three brand-new tickets were fluttering under my wipers.

I was, of course, enraged. First, I was sure that my car (which, it turned out, was a nose into the crosswalk – but a very small nose, at best) was being targeted for being an out-of-state vehicle. But much worse than that was the idea that I could be hit three times while I slept.

The tickets, which were timed for 11 PM, 2 AM and 5 AM, were each for a fair amount of money. So, gearing up for battle, I resolved to fight at least the second two.

I sent in a scathing letter, sarcastically asking why the police department didn't just stand outside my car all night and issue a stream of tickets, while they were at it. The only response I got, however, was a storm of silence – and extra fines for not paying the tickets.

I caved, eventually, and paid the fines, but years later I still resent it. And what I now know is that the cops were, in a way, being even sneakier than I had originally thought.

Why? Because at least at the time of this writing, it's the Parking Bureau's policy to dismiss "repeat summonses" if they are within three hours of each other. By timing the tickets at three-hour intervals, the cunning ticketers were closing the door to my obvious defense.

The "repeat summonses," defense, if you can swing it, is one of the best. Got a few overzealous cops writing you overlapping tickets? No problem – just point out the times on the tickets and watch the extra fines vanish.

But there are at least a few catches.

## Catch #1: It won't always work with meters

It isn't a hard and fast rule, but generally, if you get hit by an "expired meter" violation and then get hit again later, you probably won't get the second ticket dismissed due to a repeat summons.

The reason for this is that meters have maximum times allowable (see the separate section later regarding meters). So if your maximum permitted time is an hour and you get a ticket (again) two hours later, at least some judges will view this as a different event, and a valid summons.

Still, if it's your best defense – don't be afraid of using it. You might get a judge that either disagrees with the above or is just plain careless. If you don't play, you won't win.

## Catch #2: If the first ticket is defective they'll get you on the second

Let's say that you got the tickets for parking in a hand-icapped zone — a whopping fine. But the tickets are within an hour of each other. So, right off the bat, you know that you can get the second one dismissed. But then you look at the first ticket and find a technical de-fect. Jackpot, right? Both tickets dismissed and you can laugh all the way to the bank.

Not so fast. Nothing in the policy of dismissing re-peat tickets mandates that the judge has to dismiss the second (or third or whatever number) ticket. Send in both tickets and what will happen is that the judge will knock out the first — defective — one, and you'll be left with the later one that's still valid.

Is there any way around this? Well, I'm not crazy about helping someone who parks illegally in a handi-capped zone, but if it's just a regular parking offense, here's a thought that might (no guarantees) work.

The trick would be to move quickly on the second ticket — and only send in that ticket. After all, you could be de-ciding to pay the first one. You may not even realize that it's de-fective. Wait until the second ticket is dismissed (they won't dismiss the first one, or at least

> Great Spirit, help me never to judge another until I have walked in his moccasins.
>
> – Sioux Indian Prayer

they shouldn't, since you haven't asked for a hearing on it), and only then send in the first, defective, ticket. And make your defense on that ticket only about the tech-nical defect. Do that and you really ought to be able to laugh all the way to the bank. (And while you're on the way, make sure to pick up a few extra copies of this book to give to your friends.)

And, finally:

## Catch #3: Beware of different violations

This one is a technical sneakiness. Sometimes a car is parked in a way that it violates more than one section of the traffic rules. Unfortunately, each violation is a separate offense – so even if you get two or more tickets within three hours, every single one of them could still be valid.

A good example of this is if you park in a crosswalk that is also next to a pedestrian ramp. Double trouble, any way you slice it. Similarly, you should be aware that having a front plate missing (or improperly displayed) is a separate offense from a rear plate with the same problem.

Which brings us to the last point about repeat summonses:

## Status summonses are easier to get dismissed

A status summons is one that relates to the car itself, rather than to where it's parked (or stopped). Examples of this would be a car with no inspection or registration sticker, or one with broken equipment or license plates not displayed. For these violations, if you get repeat summonses anytime in the same day the repeat ones will be dismissed (but note catch #2 above, about defects). On top of this, if you get a repeat ticket within seven days, you're still in luck: You'll only pay one ticket at full price; the rest will be extremely reduced – generally, to $20 each (Of course, don't forget to send them in asking for this).

All in all, a great defense to be able to use.

## Recap: The Least You Need to Know

- Repeat Summonses within three hours of each other will get dismissed – you'll only have to pay the first.
- Catch #1: it won't always work with meters.
- Catch #2: if the first ticket is defective, they'll get you on the second.
- Catch #3: beware of different violations.
- Repeat summonses on status violations get dismissed if within 24 hours; and reduced if within 7 days.

# 8. It's Not My Car – Stolen, Sold or Borrowed Vehicles, Stickers or License Plates

## Stolen Vehicles

It's so sad that it's almost funny. The bastards stole your car, maybe even right from your driveway, and now – surprise! – you find out that thieves don't respect parking laws any more than moral ones. And you, the sweet innocent, get the parking ticket. Life just isn't fair, is it?

Well, no, it isn't. But take heart. The question of divine justice may be a philosophically entangled argument, but a stolen vehicle claim is refreshingly straightforward. And no sane parking judge will expect you to ante up the cash on behalf of the thief who parked in the wheelchair spot.

At least, that is, if you can *prove* that your car really was stolen.

And that, my friend, is at the crux of the "stolen vehicle" defense. Was your car really stolen? Or are you like the joker who claims that thieves took his car and, lo and behold, the thieves re-parked it on the next street over?

Let's look at this a bit more carefully. You wake up one day and your car has vanished. The first thing you do, probably, is to call the City to check if, for some insane reason, it was towed. But, alas, the City knows nothing about it; and the car is nowhere to be found. So you approach the police. And they have you fill in a "stolen vehicle report" and give you a copy. It ought to be obvious – but *hang on to your copy*. Hang on to it, even if the police do a great job and find your car three days later.

The reason is that although it isn't technically necessary, if at any time you need to submit the claim that your car was stolen, the parking ticket judge will be actively looking to see that document.

But just because you have a stolen vehicle report, that doesn't automatically mean you're in the clear. After all, some of the parking fines out there are pretty stiff, and there are people who are not above filing a false stolen vehicle report, figuring it's worth doing to beat the ticket(s) they have.

When we see a stolen vehicle claim, we do some sleuthing of our own. We check DMV records, and we check your history of other summonses. Is this your favorite defense? Have you used it eight times, just this past year? We'll also check out the location of those tickets. Are they a little too near your office or your home – a tad too coincidentally? How long did it take you to file your claim with the police? Is the parking ticket for Monday and you filed a claim the following

Friday? You'd be surprised at how many people try to "back-claim" a stolen car, just to avoid paying parking tickets.

Finally, don't tell us that your car was stolen, if what you really mean is that it was borrowed.

## Borrowed Vehicles

It happens all the time. Your teenager took the car when you weren't even home, and before you know it, there are seven notices magically appearing in your mailbox, because naturally your darling child "forgot" to tell you about all of the tickets he accumulated.

This is another of those "life isn't always fair" situations, but here, sadly, you don't get too many breaks. You can try to go for the sympathy vote and hope that the judge reduces the fine on the ticket(s) (or at least throws out the late penalty, on the grounds that you never got the first ticket), but the fact is that unless your kid took the car and you sicced the police on him and had him arrested, your car was not, technically, stolen. And the law slaps the parking fine on the owner of the vehicle – even if it was being driven by the cutest daughter in your flock.

Which brings us to another, similar type of claim: A vehicle that you sold or otherwise transferred ownership of.

> Dear Sir/Madam,
>
> I know that I deserved the two tickets that I received for parking in the handicapped spot. And I truly intended to pay for them. Only I left both tickets in my glove compartment and my car was then stolen. I feel that the only fair thing now would be for the thief to pay for these tickets.
>
> Please dismiss the tickets and fine the thief when you find him. And when you do, tell him to return my car!

## Sold or Transferred Vehicles

If you really sold your car and then that car got a ticket –
you're in the clear. All you have to do, again, is prove
your claim. Have exact dates available and send or bring
in copies of all the documents. In particular, show us
that your insurance on the car was canceled or transferred. Or, if possible, show us that the car is now registered in another state.

On the list of things to tell us, though, do not – repeat, not – rely on merely telling us that you surren-
dered your plates to the DMV. It's not that we won't
check the DMV records anyway (we will). It's the fact
that giving in your plates is not solid evidence that the
car was truly transferred. You could be trading them
in for any number of reasons, including getting vanity
plates or for the purposes of reregistering your car in
another state.

Still, if the sale was what's known as an "arm's-length
transfer" – that is, it's clearly being transferred to some
third party who isn't related to you – proving your claim
ought to be straightforward.

But what if you're that parent who's simply had
enough of paying off your son's tickets? So you say to
him, "to hell with it, it's now *your* car." Are you now in
the clear?

Not exactly. To begin with, you're probably still the
owner of record. So there's not likely to be any documentation that you can show us. You're probably also
still paying the insurance bill – more paper that points
to you as the owner. And if it's a son or daughter that
still lives at home, the ticket may have been issued close
to your residence. That stake through your heart just
keeps getting longer, doesn't it?

Even if the judge believes you (he or she may have teenagers of their own), there's still not much we can do for you if you don't make it easy for us. Legally, the car is probably still yours. And what's more, you ought to know it. After all, if you owe money and the bank wants to put a lien on the car, what's stopping them? And if your son turned around and sold it, what new owner would settle for your kid's word that it's his to sell?

So – if you really meant it, it's truly not your car, go the extra distance and fill out the paperwork. That way, the tickets will come in your kid's name to begin with. Let it be *their* headache, remember?

> There are three kinds of lies: lies, damned lies, and statistics.
>
> – Benjamin Disraeli

Same goes for any other kind of gift that you want to make of your vehicles. Do the paperwork, or be resolved to have a tough time proving that the car isn't still your own.

## Stickers & License Plates

It's pretty rare for stickers to be stolen in the conventional sense (and see the section later on specific sticker violations or mix-ups). But it is possible for someone to fraudulently use your sticker if they get their hands on it. If this does happen, you'll have a tough time proving it (especially if the car is a similar make and color), but anything is possible. Bring in any documents you have and argue your case with passion. Be sure to file a report with all the authorities you can – at a minimum, alert the police and the DMV, and request new stickers.

If it's your plates that were stolen, and the judge finds your claim credible, then your tickets will be thrown out without further ado. As before – credibility is the key to success.

There is, however, one caveat. If your front plate, for example, was stolen and you decide not to drive your car until you can replace it (the lawful thing to do), you still, believe it or not, have a problem: you have a duty to replace it quickly. The worst case I saw of this type was of a guy sent over to serve in Iraq, whose plate was stolen. His parents couldn't get the DMV to replace the plate without their son on hand (they needed his signature, at the least). And meanwhile, the car kept getting slapped with violations. This was one case that I took to a senior judge, because I wanted to do something for them. But, to my chagrin, the judge just proclaimed that they had a duty to get the car off the street!

So much for mercy.

To make matters worse, when it comes to plates, you can be screwed twice over if the thieves only stole one of your plates – and you mistakenly thought that you only legally needed one plate. First, you get hit by all of the tickets the thieves are getting in their car with your plate. And then the good 'ole traffic cops get you too – because you still have a duty to replace the plate quickly.

There is *some* good news, however. For all these ownership claims, even if your ticket is already in judgment, if we believe you that the car/plate was stolen, you will get the ticket dismissed. This is a better deal than if you have, say, a good "authorized vehicle" defense which you've sat on for so long that the ticket is now in judgment (for more on tickets in judgment, see Chapter 27).

**Recap: The Least You Need to Know:**

- To use a stolen or sold vehicle/plate/sticker defense you must be *credible.*
- Documents help!
- A borrowed vehicle is not a stolen one.
- Selling your car to your child only works if it's a *real* sale.
- You must replace stolen plates *quickly.* And provide the documentation that you did.

# 9. The Sign Was Confusing/Wrong/ Illegible/Missing/Too Far Away

**The Sign was Confusing**

The letter was the first that I read that morning – at the top of the pile – and I didn't have to read far to know that the nice-sounding couple from Florida was screwed.

They had come in for a quick visit to see their daughter graduate from college. To celebrate, they bought tickets to a Broadway show and drove down to midtown New York to wine and dine before being entertained. Driving around the heavily trafficked area, they finally found a few spots that looked open for parking. Dutiful citizens, they read the signs carefully, noted the one that proclaimed "Pay at the Muni meter" and dutifully paid for the spot. They even, they professed to me, were meticulous about placing their meter receipt prominently on the top of their dashboard, easily visible to any parking cop.

So why, they wailed, were they slapped with a whopping $115 fine? Was it because they had out-of-state plates on their car, they wondered?

Alas, what the couple didn't understand was evident to me from the ticket itself. They were victims of the "confusing signs syndrome" – that peculiar affliction in which you lose good money due to bad signage. And the signs in midtown New York are particularly notorious for their deceptiveness.

Take the sign that the Floridians got plastered by. The sign – or signs, to be more accurate – prohibited any standing except for commercial vehicles. Fair enough. But beneath that clear sign there were signs showing all kinds of times that parking was prohibited for anyone, *plus* signs saying that meter parking was available, between certain times, and that one should pay at the Muni meter and display the receipt. The signs are a veritable mishmash of confusion that seems designed to fool innocent tourists (most New Yorkers would probably know that finding any on-street parking in Midtown is far too good to be true).

Is it any wonder that they got hit by a ticket?

The first time that I saw one of these cases (on my first day on the job; they are that frequent) I approached a senior judge with a plea on behalf of the poor schmo who was being taken for $115. Was there nothing I could do? Couldn't I, at least, reduce the fine?

No way, she answered me. It's a "no standing" zone – and the policy of the Parking Bureau is to just about never reduce a "no standing" violation.

But the signs were confusing, I argued.

"Confusing?" She answered. And this part, I remember verbatim: "They're terrible. *I* don't know what those signs say. And I work here."

"And the fine?" I persisted.

"Full fine," she said, sighing. And she left, to instruct another new judge on the vagaries of the City's parking policies.

So it was with great reluctance that I wrote the guilty verdict for the couple from Florida. I even, if I remember correctly, wrote the judgment in the driest language possible, to conceal any personal feelings of shame that I felt for not being able to at least mitigate the fine.

All of which may clue you in to the fact that just because parking signs can be genuinely confusing, that may not be of much help to you when fighting your ticket.

So what *can* you do when faced by confusing signs?

> This is New York, and there's no law against being annoying.
>
> – William Kunstler, lawyer

To start with, don't feel bad that you're confused. One of my favorite letters that I ever read as a parking judge began "I am an M.D. and my husband is a professor and we could not understand the signs." This woman then went on to explain that they had hunted down a traffic cop, and asked him to explain it to them. The cop, whom she described as "friendly and polite" examined the sign post for a few minutes before declaring "you have to be a rocket scientist to figure it out." And then – incorrectly – told them to park there.

So don't feel bad – and as I've said before – don't rely on a passing police officer. If I had a nickel for every time someone fought a ticket saying "the officer read the sign wrong," I would have an awful lot of nickels (maybe even enough to buy a coffee from Starbucks).

And for heaven's sake, don't use the "new immigrant" approach, explaining that you don't read English well.

It might get you a passing thought of sympathy – but it won't get you off the violation.

So what *should* you do? You should fight the ticket in person. You'll probably still lose – a sign that you find confusing is still a valid legal rule, after all. But you have at least a decent chance that the judge hearing your case will be genuinely understanding of your plight; enough to possibly bend policy and reduce your fine. And if you can't make it in person, you may want to try claiming that the sign was just plain wrong. It isn't, of course, but you never know – maybe the ticketing officer was confused too and wrote the wrong thing on the ticket.

Which brings us to a different defense: what if the officer really *did* write the wrong sign on the ticket?

## The Sign is Wrong

As a general rule, if the cop who wrote your ticket wrote the wrong sign – and therefore the wrong violation – then congratulate yourself, because you're off the hook. After all, you're being ticketed for violating a specific rule, and the rule (sign) that's written on the ticket flapping under your windshield is not the one you violated.

On the other hand, if your defense is that the sign was written correctly on the ticket but was "wrong" in some other way, things are not usually so sunny.

Here's how things work. On the one hand, the Parking Bureau doesn't want to find you guilty for a "wrong" sign. On the other hand, "wrong" is usually narrowly interpreted. Thus, we would get defenses by people who claimed that the sign on the corner was wrong because the angle of the arrow printed on the sign was pointing to the "wrong" street. Signposts being somewhat susceptible to the forces of nature (and rowdy teenagers), it's not hard to believe that a sign near a corner got turned around 90°. But please, don't make arguments that defy common sense. A turned-around sign is not suddenly referring to a street 12 feet away.

Similarly, a defense that the City put the sign on the "wrong side of the street" is equally silly. Of course, we're sure that you know better. And if they only elected you mayor, the city would be running smoothly in no time. And, of course, as judges, we do know that the city often puts signs in stupid places.

> To Honored Judge Sir:
>
> I can't read English good but sign say I can park here. My sister lives in building next door, witch in Queens and we park there always. Please throw ticket away. Cop is crazy.

But so what? Would traffic flow improve if the sign was on the other side of the street? Sure. Should someone inform the right people, maybe grease the right pockets, and have that pesky sign removed? Absolutely. But in the meantime, do you really think that this is a good strategy for fighting your ticket? The only time that I ever saw anyone come even *close* to winning with this approach was on a ticket that a guy received for violating a temporary sign that was put up due to construction. And he claimed (with pictures to back it up) that the construction was really down the block. Even then, he lost his fight, because the temporary sign was put up legally, according to all the rules – even if the cop who did it didn't know the end of a cement truck from a tricycle.

But what if the cop really did screw up and the sign was wrongly stated on your ticket? If the sign said "No Parking on Mondays and Thursdays" and the cop wrote up the ticket as "No Parking on Mondays and Fridays"?

You might think that this is just a minor detail – what's in a day? Especially if you got ticketed on a Monday. But in truth, it's your "get out of this ticket free" card, with only one hitch – you must prove your case.

This might be a good time to explain that most cities keep records of which signs are put up on which streets. But these records are often cumbersome to work with, or even dead wrong. There are just too many streets and too many signs and too many frequent changes for records to be absolutely reliable. So in New York, for instance, when judges get a defense that claims that the cop wrote down the wrong sign, we check the computer system to see which signs were (supposedly) erected there.

Doing this type of a check, I can assure you, is a pain in the neck. For one thing, it involves logging onto another system, which takes a couple of minutes. And sometimes the system is down. And then we have to check the whole street for each sign that was put there. This generally involves looking through many screens of annoying data. Finally, we have to double-check everything, because there are usually so many signs indicated on the system that it's easy to miss something. All in all, it's all too easy for us to make a mistake here. Or to just get lazy and decide the case based only on your testimony – which looks awfully thin if you haven't included any photographic evidence.

This is precisely what happened to a friend of mine. He parked on a street that indicated "no parking" from 9:30 AM and received a ticket that showed the sign saying "no parking" from 8:30 AM. That is, the cop wrote down the wrong information about the sign – and gave him an undeserved ticket. Figuring that he had a straightforward case, he mailed in his defense without any supporting evidence; just his claim alone. To his shock, he eventually got back a verdict of guilty, with the judge deciding that his claim was "unpersuasive" (a word that judges tend to like, by the way, since it sounds nicer than saying "liar, liar, pants on fire!"). Whether or not the judge in this case bothered to check the sign records in the computer, we'll never know. But there's no doubt that if you want to ensure that you beat this type of ticket, you'll be better off including pictures (also see later in this section about the proper way to take pictures so that judges will be convinced by them).

### The Signs were Illegible/Missing/Far Away

What if the problem is that the sign was completely illegible? Or even outright missing in action? Or what if you just didn't see any sign because it was all the way down the block?

Let's take the case where the signs were illegible. This isn't too uncommon, at least in New York, where signs are defaced all the time by black spray paint or graffiti. If the signs really were illegible, then you ought to have a good case, at least in theory. After all, how are you supposed to know what not to do? But in practice, this is often a tough defense to win. The reason is that in order to win, *every* sign on the entire block has to be completely unreadable. On both sides of each sign. And, of course, you have to prove it. Which means plenty of pictures, taken properly (see later in this section).

Unless the kids vandalizing the signs were extremely thorough, you're out of luck. Because the law in New York is that even *one* sign on a block is sufficient. Even for a very long block. (Of course you could try carrying a can of black spray paint around and doing the job yourself – but that would, obviously, involve breaking the law more seriously than just getting a parking violation. Then again, maybe if you have a few cans of paint with you, you can get a group of irate pedestrians to help you out with the task (God knows there are enough New Yorkers out there angry about their parking tickets…)

But since I can't, obviously, recommend that…let's move on and talk about cases where the sign is missing. To win these, you again have to prove that *all* the signs were missing. This can really suck, in practice. There was one case that I had in which someone protested a ticket that he received right outside a hospital. He had arrived to undergo some medical tests, parked close to the hospital's entrance and searched in vain for a sign telling him what to do. He even, so he claimed, walked a solid forty or fifty feet in each direction, just to be on the safe side. Which, in all fairness, sounds like it ought to be enough. Unfortunately, though, a quick check of our system showed that there was one sign on the block disallowing his parking. Only because it happened to be a peculiarly long block, the sign was a full 200 feet away! Hardly a rational or fair distance to expect a man to walk before undergoing a medical test. But there it was: the law of the land. The most I could do for the gentleman was to reduce the ticket as much as I could. Which still put him out over $50. Ouch.

So, to recap – missing signs are great, but only if they're truly missing. If they're "merely" far away, the best you can hope for is that the judge will use his or her discretion wisely and at least mitigate your fine.

Unfortunately, the all-too-common plea of "I didn't see the sign – help, please!" can't help but fall on (at least partially) deaf ears. Of course, if any of you are planning on running for office, this could be a good issue to push for change. The law *ought* to read that each sign shouldn't be valid once you get farther away than 100 feet. But, hey, that's just my opinion.

## Some Other Complaints We Hear

Finally, I should mention a few general complaints that ticket-holders often air, but that don't win much more than a glance of sympathy from any self-respecting parking ticket judge.

The most obvious are the complaints about the efficacy of the signs. Ticket-fighters proclaiming that the sign "just doesn't work in that location" or that "the signs impede traffic flow rather than improve it" are just plain whiners. Did the sign(s) bother you before you got the ticket? Good – then speak up to your local politician. What do you expect *us* to do? Have the sign removed and retroactively void your ticket?

Evidently, many parking ticket warriors expect just that. The number of people who write in "please have the signs replaced" is actually staggering. So, for the record: parking judges have no control over parking signs. We probably ought to, and God knows it would make the job more interesting. But, alas, we have no such power. Sad, but true. Then again, maybe it's just as well. Who knows how many *more* people would ask, as one lady did, "please send me a letter allowing me to park in that spot, regardless of the sign, due to my ongoing need of emergency therapy following my husband leaving me (!)." Can you believe that? I was sorely tempted to grant her request (despite the futility of it) just to reward her sheer chutzpah.

Also hugging the top of the list of general complaints that we hear too often: "I didn't get any notice that the signs had changed." Truth is, I feel for these people. They've been parking in the same spot for years. Suddenly, the City wakes up and labels the street an emergency snow route, or changes the days that it cleans, and bingo, the signs change. And the poor ticketholder just doesn't notice. So they park the way they always did – but get slapped with a ticket.

Trouble is, the City doesn't owe you any more notice than the sign itself. It would be nice if they would put up posters, in bright colors, warning residents of a sign change – but until someone in power decides to institute such a policy, we have no choice but to shrug off the "no notice" defense.

And finally, for some reason, sign violations always seem to bring out all the jokers who send in long lawyerly-type letters claiming that such and such sign is unconstitutional. Or otherwise illegal. Truly, don't even get me started about these kinds of letters. Just don't bother, okay? Trust me.

And now, as promised earlier, here's:

Your Honor:

The ticket presented by the officer lacks proper due process as is required under constitutional law because the officer just left the summons under the wiper, which is not proper or personal service and is not a fair and just way of giving notice to a defendant of a crime committed. It also surely violates the fourth, fifth and sixth amendments of the U.S. Constitution, particularly with regards to unlawful searches, as the police must have done to determine what pieces of equipment were missing. Plus, it goes against State Constitutional law and State legislation and public policy regarding equity...

## How to Take Pictures that Will Help You Win

Every day hundreds, even thousands, of people send or bring in pictures to help themselves win their cases. And every day many of them lose – just because they didn't take the pics correctly.

So, how do you take photos that will help you win?

To start with, send in more than just the photo.

I didn't have many pet peeves as a judge, but the one thing that drove me right up the wall were tickets that were mailed in without so much as a word of defense or any explanation, and sporting nothing more than a poor-quality picture of *just a sign*.

I'm serious. I would check the envelope and ticket for hidden clues – to no avail. And the picture itself showed literally *just* the sign. Not even the sign-post. No possible way of locating where the picture was taken or whether the officer writing the ticket could have been mistaken. Hell, there was often no way of knowing why the person sent in a picture of that type of sign to begin with. Was it meant to show what the "real" sign said? Or was it what that sign *should* have said, according to this ticket-fighter? Or did he just think it was a pretty picture?

In that type of case, even the words "sign wrong" in a letter to the judge would have been helpful, albeit not hugely. At least it would have been obvious that he was actually making a defense.

So, obviously, just sending in a picture of the offending sign is not good enough by half. But there are also plenty of well-meaning people who send in photos of the sign and their car – or the sign next to the address

where they got the ticket. Perfectly reasonable, you
might say. And it is. But it *still* isn't the right way to fight
your ticket and here's why: in the first case, you could
have moved your car after getting the ticket and only
then taken the picture. And in the latter case, even if
the sign next to the address is referring to something
which helps you, that doesn't indicate that there isn't
a *different* sign saying another thing – which hangs
you – just out of sight.

So how do you fight a ticket using photos?

By photographing the entire street, corner to corner.

It's a pain, it's true. And in a perfect computer world,
the systems that the judges check would all be instantly
updated and reliable. But since we're all living in the real
world, where it's always smarter to make things clearer
to those who are judging us, this is what you need to
do to win: take pictures of the whole street. Make sure
that the address where you got the summons is easily
readable (if at all possible) in your photos, and if there's
a sign that you're claiming is wrong or illegible, take
pictures of *both sides* of that sign.

When you're finished with all that, take out a clean
piece of paper, get out a pen and a ruler and sketch out
a rough diagram: show us where the street is and where
your car was parked. A map isn't really necessary, legally – but it's never yet hurt.

And if you *really* want to be creative, you can always
do what one guy did and send in aerial pictures of the
whole neighborhood. Complete with satellite pictures
to match. That, at least, got a chuckle.

## Miscellaneous Information

Finally, here are a few other things to know about fighting sign-related tickets.

First off, you ought to know that if you didn't follow my advice from above, and you sent in pictures that don't show every sign on the street, all may not be lost. In theory at least, when a judge sees a reasonable defense and there's just some evidence missing (such as a few more photos), the judge should adjourn the summons (usually for thirty days) to give you a chance to send in additional evidence – the pictures you should've sent in to begin with. In practice, however, it's a crap shoot. Fact is, some judges just don't like adjourning tickets. They know that the paperwork gets messy, they doubt that your defense will really pan out, or perhaps they just don't like to seem wishy-washy. One senior judge that I remember as being bright but impatient once told me that she never adjourns a summons – on principle. "My job is to make a decision – and that's what I do," she declared. Another judge, however, had the exact opposite approach. "These are expensive tickets," she said gently, "I like to give people every opportunity to defend them."

So – life in a nutshell. Some people are harsher than others. This is even more true if you decide to fight this type of ticket in person. At a live hearing most judges are loath to adjourn if they don't have to. So if you brought in pictures that don't prove your case completely, only *some* judges will let you come back with more photos another time. Of course, some

> Dear Sir,
>
>     Not only is this ticket unfair, but the cop broke my windshield wiper putting down the ticket. You owe me $20. Enclosed is the original bill.

judges will simply believe your testimony and dismiss the ticket, maybe after asking you a few questions. But the majority, I'd wager, will assume that the computer system is accurate and that you didn't really check out every single sign on the street – because how many people even know that they're supposed to? This is one uphill battle that you're fighting.

Lastly, since there are always some people who want to know this: the one-sign-per-block rule really *is* the law; it's not just some rule that the judges made up. Check out Section 4–08(1)(i) of the Traffic Rules of the City of New York if you're really interested. The language used defines a block as "the area of sidewalk between one intersection and the next," and one sign per block suffices.

### Recap: The Least You Need to Know:

- If the sign confused you, maybe the officer was confused too and got it wrong. Best bet – fight this one in person, at a live hearing.
- If the sign on the ticket is wrong – you win. But only if you can prove it. So take pictures. Lots of pictures.
- Only one sign on a block is legally necessary – which explains why defenses based on the sign being missing in action, illegible or too far away are so difficult to win.
- When taking pictures, photograph the whole street, corner to corner, and include a sketch diagram, if you can, of where your car was parked.

## 10. I Paid the Damn Thing Already

You're in luck. If you've already paid your ticket but you keep getting notices, you don't even need to see a judge. What you're experiencing is one of those oh-so-annoying computer mess-ups that drive us all crazy. An administrative mistake that can be taken care of (eventually), especially if you have a copy of your check or whichever other payment method you used. Just call 311 and follow their directions, or go down to the office and make a nuisance of yourself until it's all taken care of. Fortunately, for this one you don't need me.

## 11. The Ticket Should be Dismissed in the Interests of Justice

You'll almost never see a judge agree to it, but there does exist a defense that is a kind of catchall for really good excuses that don't fall into any other category – and that is the defense that the ticket must be dismissed in the "interests of justice." I myself only applied this law once – to deal with a case of some tickets that respondents had sent in but somehow had been waylaid and forgotten for over three years – and then suddenly showed up on my desk. Even then I used it only reluctantly, knowing that someone higher up was undoubtedly going to question me about it. In fact, I took an informal survey one day, asking at least fifteen judges if they had ever used this defense to dismiss a summons – and not one said yes.

So why am I telling you about it? Because it's on the books, and if all else fails – especially if you're at a live hearing where you might fluster the judge – you can point out that if the judge *really* thinks that "it's unfair, but what can I do?" that there *is* a solution to his quandary – he can dismiss your ticket in the interests of justice. Sure, he might give you a strange look for asking, but it's worth a try, anyhow.

# 12. I Belong to the Press

If you're a journalist, you probably already know that as a member of the fourth estate you enjoy special parking privileges when you're covering a story. But what you probably don't know is that the Parking Bureau likes to interpret those privileges so narrowly that the plain language of the Parking Bureau's own written policies gets warped.

But let's back up a bit.

Before you can receive any press privileges at all you need one of two things: either a press license plate ("NYP"), or a valid press permit that you display when you park. Armed with these, you can park not only in areas reserved for the press but also in all "no parking" zones and "no standing/trucks loading" zones, for up to three hours, if you're actively covering a "news assignment."

In fact, you can park even longer if the first hour you were there was considered legitimate and the space then changed to being a prohibited area – and you couldn't move your car because of the nature of the news assignment. For example, if your news conference was scheduled for 11 AM, and you parked at 10:30 (in order to go to the conference) in a zone which turns into a "no standing" zone at 11:30 or later, and the news conference went on past 11:30 – you're still safe. The trick here is that you have to be there for a full hour before the zone changes into a prohibited zone.

All you need to do to get your ticket dismissed in these cases is to send in a letter on the right kind of letterhead (i.e. one from a legitimate news organization), signed by the editor, explaining the circumstances. And this ought to work for any "news assignment."

If you're covering "breaking news" then you have even more leeway. You still can't park at a hydrant, or in a bus or fire lane, or double park, but in the absence of an allowable space at the curb, you can park just about anywhere else – even in "no stopping" and "no standing" zones. This is even better than it sounds, because not only emergencies qualify as "breaking news." Unscheduled news conferences count too. (Scheduled press conferences, however, don't count, no matter how exciting or "new" the story is).

So what's the hitch? Simply this: despite the fact that the rules judges are given to adjudicate by clearly differentiate a regular news assignment from breaking news, and clearly give regular news assignments the parking privileges I mentioned above, in at least one case that came my way the senior judges all ruled that a vehicle covering a regular news assignment couldn't park in a "no standing/trucks loading" zone. In other words, they effec-

> Our decisions always have to pass the "front page of the Post" test. Every guilty verdict has the potential to embarrass us...
>
> – comment by a senior judge to the author

tively ruled that only "breaking news" stories get press privileges.

If I sound irritated, it's only because I remember the day that I first encountered this quite clearly. The defense came in by mail, and I saw that it came from a legitimate press organization and had all the elements it needed, down to the press clipping of the event that the journalist had later filed. I ruled in the journalist's favor and passed the judgment along for review by a senior judge, not giving the matter any more thought. Later that day, the senior judge passed it back to me, with a note saying that I was wrong. Never being one to meekly accept a superior's judgment, I took the ticket, along with a copy of the rules regulating press permits, back to the senior and argued with him. He listened to me politely (this particular senior was always extremely professional), promised to look at it again – and came back an hour later saying that all the seniors agreed that only "breaking news" counted. Defeated, I was left with no choice but to rewrite the judgment, this time finding the respondent guilty, against my own better judgment. The worst part of it for me was that the judgment went out into the world with my name on it. And although we're only talking about a parking ticket, not a life sentence, I still feel queasy that a small injustice was done – with my signature.

So what does this mean to you, gentle reader?

Only this: Now that you know what the verdict *should* be and what the verdict *might* be, you are armed with the only real commodity that I can give you: knowledge. My advice, then, is as follows. Assuming that you don't just have your organization deal with it for you,

you should always fight these tickets in person. The fact is, it's harder for a person to rule against you – even a hardened parking ticket judge – when you're right there in front of them arguing that the law is really on your side. Just make sure to be polite when you're pointing out that the judge is wrong.

Incidentally, there's nothing in the law that limits press privileges to only full-time staff. If you're a free-lancer, and you've managed to procure a press permit from the City – go right ahead and use it. Just make sure that when you come in with your defense, you bring in a letter from the editor that assigned you the story. Your own word generally won't suffice (sorry).

### Recap: The Least You Need to Know:

- With press plates or a press permit you can park in "no parking" and "no standing/trucks loading" zones when covering news assignments.
- When covering "breaking news" you get more lee-way.
- You can never double park – even for breaking news.
- Always fight these tickets in person and be prepared to argue the law.

# 13. Handicapped Permits

Handicapped violations are the most expensive parking tickets that are given out, and anyone with even a slight amount of compassion should be cheerful about that. Unfortunately though, not everyone who has a handicapped permit realizes that the law in New York City is trickier than it first appears.

Take the case of Mrs. Jones. Mrs. Jones was disabled due to a bout with polio as a child that left her legs unable to function properly. She wasn't very mobile, but her car was outfitted with a hand-operated device that allowed her to work the pedals without the use of her feet. She lives in New York State, but not New York City, and has a handicapped permit from the State. Driving one day into New York City, she pulls up at a handicapped-only spot on the street, leaves her permit clearly visible on the dashboard – and takes home, later that day, a "present" from the City: a fine of nearly $200.

The case comes before a New York City parking ticket judge – who can clearly see that she's disabled – and, lo and behold, she *still* walks out (so to speak) with the ticket upheld and most likely not even reduced in fine. What happened?

83

What happened is that New York City issues its own permits for the disabled. And only those permits are valid for parking on the street in handicapped zones. If you have a State-issued permit (or, for that matter, a permit from a different State), that will still help you park at malls and other off-street sites that have handicapped-only signs, but not anywhere on the streets of New York City.

Other problems? Even if you have the right permit, you still have to make sure that your times are right. It's a frustrating and depressing sight to watch a case where the disabled person appears in front of a judge showing the right kind of permit, but he clearly didn't realize that even though he was authorized to park in that spot (and non-handicapped vehicles aren't), he still has to abide by the hours posted on the sign. If it says three hours maximum parking, for example, that restriction still applies.

It's also frustrating, as a judge, to come across well-meaning people who believe that because they're *with* someone disabled (or elderly) that they can also park in those spots. You can always drop off someone in a "no parking" spot (see the "no parking" section later for details), but you can't park in a handicapped zone simply because you feel that the person you're with can't walk far. Even if it's *you* that has the problem, you still need a valid permit. Just telling me, like one lady did, that she was having trouble walking that day, will not suffice

> **A New Yorker is a person with an almost inordinate interest in mental health, which is only natural considering how much of that it takes to live here.**
>
> **– New York Times; "New Yorkers, By the Book"**

(see the section on medical emergencies for more information).

Finally, it ought to be obvious, but if you do have a handicapped permit, please don't abuse the privilege. If you have a valid handicapped permit, and you have more than one car, your permit covers more than one vehicle. Please don't use the one that doesn't have a disabled person in it to run errands with convenient parking. Sure, it isn't likely that we'll find out about it (unless the other car was ticketed elsewhere at roughly the same time – highly unlikely), but even if you can get away with it...well, it sure ain't nice. Enough said.

## Recap: The Least You Need to Know:

- Everything about permits (see chapter 6) still applies to the disabled.
- Only New York City permits are valid for on-street parking in New York City.
- Being with a disabled person isn't sufficient; you still need a permit.

# 14. I'm a Doctor or Dentist

**Y**ou're out saving lives, mending broken bones or just plain old dispensing birth control pills. You're doing important work, work that the public has a real interest in assisting you with. And you're special. That "no standing" sign couldn't possibly pertain to *you*.

Oops. It isn't pretty, but this is New York after all. And being special is, well, ordinary. If it says not to park there, and the exceptions below don't apply – then don't park there. It's easy, really. Just follow the rules, like everyone else.

If it sounds as though I'm peeved, it's because the amount of attitude judges routinely get from doctors is rather astonishing. We get letters demanding that tickets be dismissed because "otherwise lives will be lost" – despite the lack of any evidence that the driver did anything more than park illegally while picking up a latté. Or really obnoxious letters from interns, who haven't yet passed their Boards, who demand that the ticket be thrown out because "I was up all night saving New Yorkers, and the least the City can do is let me sleep in and not move for the stupid street cleaner."

Comments like those won't help you win your case. This section, however, will.

## The Rules for Doctors and Dentists

Here's the first and most obvious rule. You're allowed to park anywhere that it says "Doctors (or Dentists) Vehicles Only." Even if you don't have "MD" (or "DDS") plates. Of course, you should have those plates – they'll make your life easier. But if you're in a different car that day, your car's in the shop or whatever – just send in proof that the car belongs to you and that you really are a doctor. Don't skimp on the proof, either. Send in a copy of your license, a letter from the hospital or clinic, or even your diploma; make it crystal clear that you're an actual doctor and then rest easy. Sorry, but physician's assistants do not get the same privileges.

The second rule is that you're allowed to park on a street adjacent to a hospital or clinic for up to three hours. This can get a bit tricky because "adjacent" does *not* include side streets, yet *does* include across the street even where a pedestrian island is breaking up the street. But if you're in any doubt as to how the law works here, you have but to look on page 91, where I've included a diagram. Incidentally, it's important to remember that this applies only to "No Parking" zones. "No Standing" and "No Stopping" zones (like fire hydrants) still apply – no matter how close to the hospital they are.

> Dear Sir/Madam,
>
> My psychologist insisted that I come over immediately for emergency therapy, due to a stressful divorce. When I arrived there was nowhere to park legally, so I had to park unlawfully in order to keep my appointment.
>
> Please dismiss this ticket – I can't handle stress very well and I have no money to pay for it!

The third rule is that even if the parking spot is no-where near a hospital or clinic, a licensed physician (sorry, no dentists this time) can park in "No Parking" zones for up to one hour, as long as they're attending a patient. This, by the way, is a literal requirement. There must be a real patient there, not a meeting about one. So a doctor's conference does not count. Also, unfortunately, this does not include a doctor making rounds in a hospital. The idea here is to help out those few doctors who still make house calls, not to help doctors on their daily routines.

As a postscript to this rule, you should know that the one-hour allowance works even if the patient you're attending comes to your office – but I almost feel as if you're better off not knowing this, because it's a trap that could leave you caught in a credibility snare. Here's the trouble: most judges simply won't believe you if you claim that you only saw *one* patient in your office. They'll assume that you are, in fact, just abusing this rule while getting a free parking space for work.

So, caveat emptor on this one – and my advice is if you're going to use this defense, present it in person, at a live hearing.

Finally, the last rule is this: medical emergency rules still apply, just like they do for everyone else. Read the chapter about having an emergency (Chapter 15) for details and bolster your case by including documentation that you're a doctor. Obviously, we all have an interest in doctors stopping their cars and helping out in a real emergency. And don't forget: just saying the words "I had a medical emergency" or some such won't cut it – be specific and tell us the whole story. Details always help!

**Miscellaneous**

To conclude, you ought to know that if you're one of the many doctors who write doctor's notes for your patients, explaining that they spent longer than expected in your office – and therefore got a ticket that wasn't their fault, like for an expired meter – this is not an excuse that really helps them. There are just too many good excuses out there for why people have to park unlawfully, and the most it might do is help to get the fine reduced – if they're very lucky. If you really want to help your patients out, give them a genuinely realistic time for when they need to arrive for their appointment and help them avoid the ticket altogether. Just a thought.

**Recap: The Least You Need to Know:**

- You can park in "Doctors Only" spots, even without M.D. plates – but you must send in good proof that you're a licensed doctor.
- Parking adjacent to a hospital is okay for up to three hours.
- You get one hour in other "No Parking" zones – if you're seeing a patient.
- Medical emergency rules still apply, same as they do for everyone else.
- Generally, mailing in your defense is the easiest way to fight these tickets. Fight it at a live hearing only if it's likely that your believability is on the line.

Section 4-08 Title 34 Department of Transportation

# Shaded areas are considered adjacent.

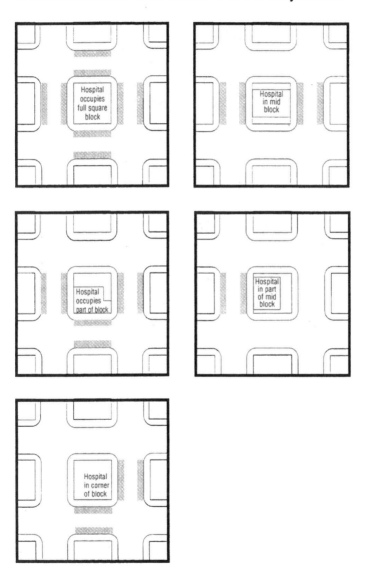

# 15. It Was an Emergency

Of all the general defenses that you can use when hit by a parking ticket, medical emergency is probably my favorite.

Of course, if you're *having* a medical emergency it's most likely no picnic for you – and a parking ticket is the absolute last thing on your mind. But once your emergency is over (and hopefully all is well) you can begin to appreciate just how great a defense a medical emergency is.

The reason that the "medical emergency defense" is so wonderful is that it's unbelievably sweeping. Parked at a fire hydrant? No problem. Left your car in a bus zone? No worries. Pulled over into a handicapped spot? "Fuhgedd-about-it." It's all good.

So what's the catch?

There is none. But before you rush out and claim that your car was parked there because of an emergency there are a few things that you'd better know. Call these mini-catches.

### Mini-Catch #1:
The emergency has to involve a human being. No joke.

As a judge I've seen people claim that they had to park at a hydrant because their cat was having kidney problems, or their kid's hamster had a broken leg and even, in one memorable case, that the pet dog was vomiting all over their car's brand-new leather interior.

None of these are what the Parking Bureau will admit were real "medical emergencies." And sure, we all know that's a bit unfair. After all, who wants dog puke all over the new car? Not to mention the grief your child will give you if the beloved family cat dies of kidney failure. But take heed: the next time that you want to tell the judge you took the handicapped spot because your bird stopped chirping or because your lizard lost its camouflaging skills – don't say that you weren't warned. A "medical emergency" it isn't.

But let's say that your emergency involves a real human being. Homo sapiens. Hell, let's say you don't even *like* animals – or that your idea of an afternoon sport is to cause a few deer to have "medical emergencies" that they won't recover from. Does that mean you're in the clear?

Not exactly.

Because your idea of an "emergency" and a parking judge's idea of an emergency don't always match.

Which brings us to:

### Mini-Catch #2:

The need to pee is not a medical emergency.

This is a fun one. A mother with a mini-van stuffed with kids pulls over into a no standing zone because no less than three of her darlings are screaming that they'll pee in their undies if they don't get relief.

Do I feel pity for her? Do I ever. But unless she can

find some other excuse, she's probably going to wish she just paid for a Laundromat instead. It's bound to be cheaper than the fine that the Parking Bureau says not to even mitigate (more on that later).

Or how about the truck driver who's been on the road all night, drowning himself in coffee that now desperately wants to escape from him? Er, better hold it in a bit longer there, mister – at least until you find somewhere legal to park. Because you're not going to get much sympathy from the judge. (Not sympathy that will help you, at any rate; however much we feel inside, we still have to uphold the law as interpreted by the City).

Or my personal favorite, mostly because the guy who wrote it tried to be a bit sneaky: The story about a patient who had urological problems (so far so good – and he even supplied a doctor's note) and he therefore had to stop to urinate immediately. Because his bladder simply couldn't hold it in. Which would have been a great defense,

> I haven't committed a crime. What I did was fail to comply with the law.
>
> – David Dinkins, New York City Mayor, answering accusations that he failed to pay his taxes

had he been driving when the urge came. But this bloke was charged with overtime parking – and he had already been parked there for 40 minutes too long when he got the ticket! Now if only the doctor had written that it often took his patient an hour to urinate…

Which brings us to the point: if you *really* can't hold it in and you must park illegally, at the very least try to park in a place where the fine is relatively light because you probably *will* be paying it.

I should add that new parking judges always feel bad

about having to uphold fines in these kinds of cases –
but it's nothing compared to:

**Mini-Catch#3:**
Pregnancy is not an automatic get-out-of-this-ticket-
free card.

Every so often a husband will write in that he had
no choice but to double park in front of his building,
because his eight-month pregnant wife needed to lie
down, pronto. And he needed to help her up the stairs.
The first time I saw this I ended up getting scolded by a
senior judge for wanting to give the guy a break.

"She needed to lie down?" The senior judge (who was a
woman) asked. "Needing to lie down isn't an emergency.
If it was a *real* emergency, the only place he would have
been double parking in front of is a hospital."

So the poor guy ended up with a whopping fine –
and my unspoken sympathy. [If he had helped her just
to the curb, I could've done something for him, as
you're allowed to drop off a passenger while double
parked, and she could have been considered a person
needing assistance to exit the car].

The next time I encountered the "pregnant defense"
was a nine-month pregnant woman who pulled over at
a bus stop because her vision blurred. Unlike the first
case, here – finally! – was a real "medical emergency."
After all, the last thing any city needs is a driver who's
feeling dizzy, or whose vision is off. And pregnant
women are more believable (sorry, guys) when it comes
to sudden spells of feeling faint.

My advice? If you're trying to get out of a ticket because you're pregnant, you're only likely to succeed if
there was something genuinely wrong – and a doctor's

note sure would help. [No guarantees, though; I know of one judge who found a husband guilty even though the doctor's note testified that his wife was busy giving birth and desperately wanted the father with her].

Speaking of doctors, I ought to mention:

## Mini-Catch #4:

Having a doctor's appointment does *not* mean it was a medical emergency.

It seems silly, at first blush, that this one is true – but there it is. Let's say that you're having a stomach problem. You call up your gastroenterologist, she says to come right over and you, grateful for the quick appointment, park wherever you can. In your state of mind, all you can think is: To hell with the fire department – there are, after all, other hydrants on the street.

So you get a ticket, plead a medical emergency and even get the M.D. to write up your whole medical history to back you up. [In some cases, I should add, the M.D. feels compelled to add in a financial hardship argument too – I've seen doctors' notes that seem to be more about complaining about not getting paid than about their patient's condition]. And you breathe easy.

Only you shouldn't. Because, fair or not, the judge is likely to tell you that any scheduled appointment, by definition, is not such an emergency that you couldn't take the time to park legally. Oops. So much for sympathy.

But don't fret too much, because doctors themselves can't always be "physicians that help themselves," due to:

## Mini-Catch #5:

Doctors don't always get off.

I deal more with this in the section devoted to doctors, but for here, let me say this: An emergency means an emergency. Pulling over to the curb to make a phone call because you're on call or visiting a patient whose disease/injury is not life-threatening or urgent just won't cut it. And, really, you don't have to be so snotty when you write in your plea. (And no, I've nothing against doctors).

Finally, let me finish up with this:

## Mini-Catch #6:

Successful medical emergency defenses are rare.

They're rare because you must convince the judge that it was a genuine emergency. Visiting a sick uncle won't do the trick. Feeling nauseous might – but will the judge believe you? A medical emergency defense is an affirmative one – which means that the burden of proof is on you to show that it really happened.

My suggestion, therefore, when claiming a medical emergency defense, is this: Add every bit of supporting evidence you can think of. A doctor's note? Definitely. Photos of the bee stings on your eyelids – why not? A newspaper clipping of how you saved the life of an auto-accident victim? Even better.

In short, when you use this defense you have in your hands a potentially powerful weapon. Use it well and genuinely – and you will prevail.

> To the Judge:
>
> Please excuse this ticket. I know that I parked in a no standing zone, but I did it because I was having an educational emergency. I am a teacher and I was running late to my class – I had to teach that class quickly! The kids will simply vanish if I'm not on time. Please, for the sake of our children – dismiss this ticket!

**Recap: The Least You Need To Know:**

- The medical emergency defense is a stellar defense for getting out of tickets.
- There are several Mini-Catches:
  - (1) The emergency must be for a human being;
  - (2) The need to go to the bathroom is not considered an emergency;
  - (3) Pregnancy is, by itself, not a sufficient defense;
  - (4) Having a doctor's appointment is not usually considered an emergency;
  - (5) Just because you are a doctor doesn't mean it's an emergency;
  - (6) A successful defense is rare – and the burden of proof is on you.
- It's always a good idea to submit a doctor's note, if you can get one.

# PART II

## THE VIOLATIONS & HOW TO DEFEND THEM:
### *If a general defense won't cut it.*

# 16. No Parking – All Types

It was a terrible case. A lady was driving with her young daughter, whom she needed to drop off at the little girl's special needs school. Her child was already eight years old, but suffered from debilitating physical and mental handicaps, and couldn't possibly just hop out of the mother's car and into the school on her own. The mother, a secretary at a small business, was late for work and with all her other troubles, she claimed that the $65 fine that she received while she took her daughter into the building (having parked in a "no parking" zone), was just too much for her. The letter that she mailed in was heartrending. And to bolster her case, the school's principal included an eloquent plea for mercy on her behalf.

The judge dealing with the case, who was sitting next to me, looked distinctly unhappy as he showed me his verdict: guilty! To my astonishment, he hadn't even reduced the fine. "I feel like a s*!@*t," he confessed, "but just yesterday, they (the senior judges reviewing his work) chewed my head off for acquitting a case just like this."

I felt sorry for my friend (not to mention the poor

mother), but what I felt most was frustration at how unnecessary getting the ticket actually was. For if the mother had only known the law, she could have avoided the whole mess altogether – by having someone ready at the curb to help her daughter. And she *still* could've pulled her car into that same spot, put it in park and helped her daughter out of the car.

Here's the scoop: "No parking" still means that you are allowed to stop your car, put it in park if you have to, drop your passengers off, and give them the time to unload their belongings – and that even includes stuff that they have in the trunk. The only two caveats are these: The whole thing must be done "expeditiously" (meaning in a reasonably quick way), and any unloading of bags or passengers can only be to the curb. That last part bears repeating: You can only unload your bags to the *curb* – not to your building (and not to your door-man's station).

Where people typically get into trouble is with the almost-impossible-to-resist temptation to move those suitcases over just a *wee* bit to the doorman, before going back for the next piece of luggage. Truth is, there probably *was* a time when the risk of getting ticketed during that extra minute was negligible; what were the odds of a cop coming by just then? But with the glut of meter maids on the prowl for parking offenses that currently defines the hunting landscape of New York City parking, the chances of getting caught has risen considerably. And if you do get that ticket, then it becomes a question of credibility; that is, whether the judge believes that you both *knew* the law (about unloading just to the curb) – *and* that you followed it meticulously.

Which brings me to my next point. If you did follow

the law, and your passengers left their stuff at the curb, or you helped your elderly mother or handicapped child out of the car but only to the curb, and you *still* got a ticket, your best bet is to fight it in person. This is important because you're going to have to persuade a skeptical judge that that's really what happened. Be prepared to tell the judge who you left your passengers with. And that the person was at the curb. It's just too likely otherwise that the judge will assume that you dropped your elderly parent off *in* the store.

But what if you *did* actually leave your car (and not just go to the curb, either), but you left someone else inside it? Is that good enough? After all, how "parked" are you, if there's a driver ready to move at a moment's notice?

This is probably one of the worst misconceptions people have. The unhappy truth is that leaving someone else in the car doesn't help you at all. Although it does, I admit, make for some very cute defenses.

> Good judgment comes from experience, and experience – well, that comes from poor judgment.
>
> **– Cousin Woodman**

Like the husband who explained that he "just ran inside to McDonald's to get dinner for my wife, who was in the car, and hadn't eaten in hours." Or the twenty-two year old who wrote in that "I left my sleeping fiancé in the car, with the engine running, to get money from the ATM; got back, got a kiss and had the moment ruined by seeing the ticket…" Not to mention the all too un-cute story of the man who grumbled that "my wife was nagging me so much about stopping for her stupid salad that if I hadn't parked there and waited for her to pick up her food, I would have had an accident out of sheer frustration." (That's the kind of case where you wonder how the guy ever got married in the first place...)

Similarly, the excuse that you only parked there briefly (even without leaving anyone in the car) rarely works successfully. I had numerous cases where the respondent wrote in something like "I was hungry, so I went for a sandwich, for not more than five minutes and when I got back..." Or the always sympathetic but unsuccessful plea that "I just *had* to go to the bathroom," followed by "and I was only there for a few minutes!" None of which really work. The most that can happen with these (and that only if you're lucky enough to get a very friendly judge) is that you'll get the fine reduced. Which can't hurt, of course, but be aware that it's a long shot. After all, almost everyone has a good or semi-good reason to park in those spots "only for a little while." Not everyone is as silly as the student who wrote in that "there was nowhere legal to park, so I had to park unlawfully."

Which reminds me, here are two more types of excuses that you ought to avoid: Any that complain about how difficult it is to find parking, and any where the judge will ask you "but why didn't you think about that beforehand?"

An example of the first kind is the one where there had been a bad snowstorm the previous day and the snow hadn't yet been cleared. Naturally, there were fewer parking spaces to be found. But it hardly follows that therefore everyone can then park their cars in forbidden zones. If anything, the city will be more likely to need those lanes clear then more than ever – to get snow-removal vehicles down the streets.

As for the second kind of excuse, my favorite is the

defense which starts with "I had to pull over because it was time to pray." With these I have to choke back a biting retort: "And was this a surprise to you? Don't you have to do that every day?"

On the other hand, an example of a *good* excuse is one which explains why you couldn't help but be parked in a prohibited area. A medical emergency (see chapter 15) is an obvious example, but the reason doesn't always have to be so extreme. For instance, I remember dismissing a street-cleaning ticket on the grounds that the owner had recently recovered from a respiratory infection (he provided a doctor's note) and since it had snowed badly the night before, and the streets were icy, the man was physically scared to go out and move his car. This seemed like a perfectly reasonable excuse to me, especially considering that the car had been parked legally overnight. Of course if he had just said that his alarm clock had failed and he couldn't get there in time, the outcome would have been "slightly" different.

And while we're on the subject of street-cleaning, or really any other time when your car was initially parked legally in a zone that then becomes prohibited (with the exception of meters, see Chapter 18), you should know that the first few minutes of the prohibited time aren't so prohibited. If you're confused by that, let me say it more simply: If the sign says "no parking" from, say, 8 AM, then you really have until 8:04 AM to move your car.

This isn't a very well-known fact, and God knows how many cops seem to enjoy writing tickets that pounce on their victims only one minute into the violation, but the (unofficial) policy of the Parking Bureau is to give you the first few minutes free. Some judges will allow you even five minutes free, but truthfully, with five minutes you're already beginning to push your luck.

There are two theories as to why drivers should be given the first few minutes free, and they're important to understand, if only to be able to know what it is, legally, that you're relying on.

The first theory is that we tend to assume that many cops will jump the gun and give out tickets (especially for something like street cleaning) a bit too early. Your defense, under this theory, is that the time on the ticket is actually incorrect, and that the sign wasn't yet in effect. Nine times out of ten, if a driver writes in saying that according to the radio it wasn't yet the time that that zone became illegal, and the violation time written on the ticket is only a few minutes away, the judge will accept the claim. Under this theory, however, if you write in that you agree with the cop – it was, in fact, 8:01 AM – but that you believe it's wrong to get a ticket "for just one minute," then you run the risk that the judge will say to you, "sorry, Bud – tough luck. A minute is still a minute." And I've seen many a senior judge do just that.

The second theory, however, is more broad – and relies on better legal legs, so to speak. This is the theory of "de minimus non curat lex" (the law disregards tiny infractions). And yes, for those of you lawyers who might wish to protest, it does apply even to parking tickets. De minimus is the legal idea that if somebody only violates the law in the most minimal way, it's not a real violation. An example would be the thief who only steals one penny from his friend. By corollary, when it comes to parking tickets, someone who parks in a "no parking" zone for only a minute or two (or possibly even four or five) has only very minimally violated the law – and it's not a real violation.

Now I know what you're thinking. I said before that an excuse that you parked in a "no parking" zone for only a few minutes won't fly. And that even taking your bags an extra few feet to the door of your building – which surely took only a minimal amount of time! – will land you in fine-paying territory. So, how can what I said before be true?

The answer is, because the language of the law when it comes to these violations is very specific – the law states that you must be "actually engaged in loading or unloading property or passengers" to get out of a "no parking" violation because you were really "standing" rather than "parking" – and loading bags to the door, rather than to the curb, is not considered, in these cases, as being "actually engaged in unloading" and hence is not considered merely a "minimal" violation.

Which isn't, I admit, a very satisfying answer.

But nevertheless, the bottom line is that what won't work in general for "no parking" zones, *will* work when the zone started as a legal spot and then morphed into a prohibited spot. Like in the case of street-cleaning.

Which means that under the de minimus theory, even if you flagrantly boast that you only moved your car at 8:01 AM, rather than 8 AM, you should be whistling your way to work, unworried about any ticket.

However, real life can sometimes be funny. I had a friend who got a ticket two minutes into the street-cleaning violation and tried to convince the cop whom he saw writing up the summons that under the de minimus theory he had every legal right to be there. The cop, unimpressed, handed him the ticket. So my friend schlepped down to a hearing, and tried to convince the judge. But the judge didn't much like that theory either, and convicted him. Finally, my friend mailed in an appeal, complete with legal sources – and last I heard, he was still waiting for justice to arrive.

The moral? You have to fight hard – even when you're dead right. And if you're anything like me, you ought to take satisfaction when you finally *do* win, because as a driver, there weren't many tickets that pissed me off more than the ones I would get right after nearly giving myself a heart attack in my hurry to get to my car on time early in the morning.

And incidentally, while we're talking about street-cleaning tickets, here's a helpful clue about those signs that say "no parking school days" and also have "no parking" during street-cleaning hours. The signs might at first blush seem to contradict each other, but they don't. What they mean is that the street-cleaning sign is in effect on days that are *not* school days, when people are allowed to park there the rest of the day.

Which brings me to a more general piece of advice: You should almost always try to avoid parking in zones that say "no parking school days." The truth is, these signs are snares for the unwary. You might be completely certain that a Saturday in the middle of the summer isn't a school day, for example, and yet still get a ticket – because that particular school holds summer school on weekends.

Ironically, the people who seem to get hit most by these tickets are teachers – especially substitute teachers. I can't begin to count how many times I read a defense that would start with: "I'm a teacher and there-

fore have every right to park there." The trouble here
is that they are confusing areas in which only Board of
Ed permit holders can park (which will have signs saying something to the effect of "only authorized vehicles
with Board of Education permits can park here" with
"school days" signs. In brief, "school days" refers to a
*time period*. And during that time "no parking" means
just what it says. So unless the sign clearly says that
your kind of permit works there – avoid the spot (for
more detailed information on permits and "authorized
vehicles only" spots, see Chapter 6).

Finally, here's a good tip when it comes to "no parking" tickets, or really *any* type of
ticket: never rely on a cop's word.
I know it seems crazy (and I've
said this before), but just because
the cop said something doesn't
make it true. I've had people say
"I got a ticket, but the cop said
'don't worry, now you can park
here all day,'" which is just plain
wrong. There are plenty of people
who ask cops for help in reading
the signs and, unfortunately, more often than not the
cops are no wiser than you are in this area. So here's a
good rule of thumb: If it sounds too good to be true, it
probably is.

Lastly, don't forget to read through Part 1 of this
book to see if any of the general defenses (available for
all tickets, not just "no parking") apply to you. A ticket
for a run-of-the-mill "no parking" zone isn't always
easy to win, but it is possible. And if nothing else, a

> Respectfully:
> These tickets are far over-
> priced. Crooked politicians drove
> up the deficit and now they want
> us to pay for it. And the tow sys-
> tem is a legalized form of car theft
> and extortion.
> Please reduce the fine to a
> sane amount.

good story will give you a shot at getting the fine reduced (for more on pleading guilty with an excuse, see Chapter 24).

### Recap: The Least You Need to Know:

- "No Parking" still allows you to unload passengers and luggage to the curb.
- Leaving someone in the car doesn't mean that your car isn't "parked".
- Parking in a "no parking" zone briefly is still going to get you convicted, most of the time.
- If it's a street-cleaning ticket however, you get the first few minutes free – so fight for it!
- Try to provide a reason why you couldn't help but park there.
- Try to avoid "school days" zones.
- Never trust a cop's word.
- Don't forget to read the rest of the book, especially Part 1, to find defenses that may work.

# 17. No Standing – All Types

If ever the city of New York made a Faustian bargain and lost its soul, the payoff by the red-horned angel was undoubtedly delivered through the revenues generated by "no standing" tickets. Put simply, these summonses are so expensive and so harshly judged that if each parking ticket judge found only three of these tickets guilty every day, their salary would be paid for – with change left over.

Officially, the City likes to say that it is so important that "no standing" zones remain free of stopped vehicles that the public interest in quality traffic flow justifies both the high initial fine and the "no mercy" policy that the Parking Bureau demands of its personnel. Unofficially, it's hard to shake the feeling that they also really, really like the cash.

So my job in this section is straightforward. If you can't find any general defense from Part 1 that will work for you, the least I can do is point out what *not* to do when you're defending against this cash-cow ticket, and how, perhaps more importantly, to avoid the next ticket altogether. Because these really are tough tickets to beat.

Let's start by explaining just what it is that you are and are not allowed to do in "no standing" zones.

> In the spider-web of facts, many a truth is strangled.
>
> – Paul Eldridge

The *one* thing that you're allowed to do in a "no standing" zone that you can't do in a "no stopping" area is to pick up and/or drop off passengers (as long as it's done "expeditiously"). But here's the tricky part: Your passengers can't load or unload any real luggage. Which means that you can't just pop open the trunk and let them throw in their gear, or watch and wait for them as they drag their oversized suitcase from the curb and wrestle it into the seat in the back.

If the bag they're carrying is small, such as a purse or a small bag of snacks, then you'll be okay. But anything more than that and you run the risk of the judge assuming that you were "loading" bags along with people.

Of course, even if you're just picking up a friend while you're standing in a "no standing" zone, there's always the risk that the parking cop giving out tickets doesn't really know the law. So if you get a ticket and you want to use this defense, make sure that you clarify to the judge that you knew the law even before the ticket arrived. Your best bet, by the way, would be to go to a live hearing in this case, and to bring your friend as a witness. Just writing in your passenger's name and even their phone number is generally not a successful route to take.

As far as other things that you're allowed to do in a "no standing" zone – well, there really aren't any. If you get out to physically assist your passenger in or out of the car, be sure to have that passenger on board when you fight the ticket. And, yes, I know it's crazy to schlep your elderly grandfather to a hearing with you, but, hey, it's $115 and counting. Maybe he could at least write a letter for you. And maybe that'll even work.

Incidentally, whatever you do, please *don't* do what one guy did, writing in that "no standing cannot be reasonably interpreted as no parking" – to justify parking his car at a bus stop (a "no standing" zone) while going for a hot dog.

The real trouble with "no standing" zones, however, is not what you are or are not allowed to do in them. It's the fact that the City doesn't really care how good your excuse is. Didn't notice the sign? They don't care. In from out-of-state, and you just stopped your car to get out and ask for directions? Tough luck. I actually had that case once – a gentleman from Florida who explained just how lost and desperate he was, and how he only left his car for two minutes. And I felt genuinely sorry for the bloke even as I was scribbling the word "guilty" on the judgment sheet.

The problem is that the Parking Bureau won't allow the judges to mitigate fines in "no standing" cases (excuse me, I mean they "strongly recommend" no mitigation, as officially there's still discretion by the judges, however little there may be in reality). The result of this draconian policy is that even really good excuses don't help.

Take excuses by taxi drivers, for example. This is one of those categories where one gets the feeling that the City doesn't much like its cabbies. After all, their whole job is to stop and pick up passengers and then drop them off somewhere – and very often that will include taking their luggage. Yet there's almost nowhere for them to legally stop for someone with luggage. Sure,

For Taxis (Section 4–11 of the Traffic Rules):

(a) **Standing.** No operator of a taxi, while awaiting employment shall stand his/her vehicle in any street except:

(1) At an authorized taxi stand.

(2) In front of fire hydrants where standing or stopping is not prohibited by signs or rules, provided that the operator remains in the operator's seat ready for immediate operation of the taxi at all times and starts the motor on hearing the approach of fire apparatus, and provided further, that the operator shall immediately remove the taxi from in front of the fire hydrant when instructed to do so by any member of the police, fire, or other municipal department acting in his/her official capacity.

(3) In the area of the Borough of Manhattan, bounded by the north side of 60th Street, the east side of First Avenue, the south side of 14th Street and the west side of Eighth Avenue, on those streets where "No Standing Except Trucks Loading or Unloading" is posted and in effect, the operator of a taxi, while waiting for a passenger, may stand for the period of one traffic signal cycle, provided that no taxi shall stand in any area where parking is restricted to diplomatic or other classes of vehicles and provided further that the operator remains in attendance at the vehicle and shall immediately remove it when instructed to do so by any law enforcement officer.

(c) Pickup and discharge of passengers by taxis, commuter vans and for-hire vehicles.

they may get lucky and have a fare waiting for them in a simple "no parking" or "no standing/trucks loading" zone (where they're allowed to stop and load), but, more often than not, cabs in New York aren't even stopping for passengers in "no standing" zones at all – they're pulling up in "no stopping" areas such as crosswalks. And then they get slapped with a ticket.

Now I have to admit that when you stop to pick

Operators of taxis, commuter vans and for-hire vehicles may, in the course of the lawful operation of such vehicles, temporarily stop their vehicles to expeditiously pick up or discharge passengers at the curb in areas where standing or parking is prohibited.

Taxis, commuter vans and for-hire vehicles, while engaged in picking up or discharging passengers must be within 12 inches of the curb and parallel thereto, but may stop or stand to pick up or discharge passengers alongside a vehicle parked at the curb only if there is no unoccupied curb space available within 100 feet of the pickup or discharge location; however, picking up or discharging passengers shall not be made:

**(1)** Within a pedestrian crosswalk.

**(2)** Within an intersection, except on the side of a roadway opposite a street which intersects but does not cross such roadway.

**(3)** Alongside or opposite any street excavation when stopping to pick up or discharge passengers obstructs traffic.

**(4)** Under such conditions as to obstruct the movement of traffic and in no instance so as to leave fewer than 10 feet available for the free movement of vehicular traffic.

**(5)** Where stopping is prohibited.

**(6)** Within a bicycle lane.

**(7)** Within horse-drawn carriage boarding areas.

someone up in a "no stopping" zone it's fair to get a ticket. Even if you are a cab driver. But there really ought to be some leeway for a cab picking up a fare with luggage from a "no standing" area, otherwise most of us would never be able to get a cab to the airport! Or, as one taxi driver asked me, after getting hit by a fine for helping a person load their luggage in a "no standing" spot, "should I just tell them to jump into the moving car?"

But as I said, good excuses rarely work here.

And if good excuses don't help, wacky ones certainly won't. Like this letter that I once found on my desk: "I was unloading my laundry – five huge bags – my weekly load, honest to God, as we have four boys. And with so much laundry, we have to do it by car. I left to load, went back to the car for the detergent – and found the ticket. Enclosed are pictures of my laundry (!!). $115 is a lot of money for laundry. Please dismiss."

And honest to God, she had included pictures of soiled clothes.

Enough said.

But if ever the City could be accused of being indifferent to its drivers' parking ticket sorrows, the prime exhibit would be the infamous "commercial meter no standing" zones. I discussed this in the "signs" section (chapter 9), but it's worth repeating: These signs are bait for the unwary. Drivers of passenger vehicles act, all too often, like sardines swimming into the trap set for them by the city sharks; the lure of cheap parking overcomes our usual caution. And once in the trap – the shark shows no mercy. If you're not a commercial vehicle, you get the full fine (these are "no standing" zones for all but commercial vehicles). Your only real hope if you get caught with one of these tickets is if you happen to have a strange kind of license plate, because I've noticed that many cops get lazy when ticking off the plate type in these tickets. So, for example, if you have a vanity plate, you might just get lucky and have your ticket dismissed because the cop checked off "passenger" as the plate type – a technical defect (check chapter 1 for other possible technical defects you can use to beat your ticket).

But otherwise, getting a "no standing commercial meter" ticket is as bad, in the City's eyes, as if you stopped and parked at a bus stop. Which, unsurprisingly, cops really don't like. As a matter of fact, I've seen some pretty lame excuses by people caught with bus stop tickets. I've had people defend themselves by saying they had just stopped to get a slice of pizza, to use their cell phones, or because "the other spots were already taken." Are these really good reasons for a bus to be unable to drop people off? Although I must admit that I caught a quick smile when one respondent claimed that he stopped at a bus stop to try to pick up a pretty girl – and that it worked. Ah, l'amour. I was tempted to write back that I would waive the fine – if they ultimately got engaged. But, alas, this suitor added in the unhelpful fact that he had helped the girl with her luggage. By admitting to having opened the trunk, the schnook had tied my hands…

Incidentally, you *can* pick up or drop off passengers at a bus stop, same as you can in other "no standing" zones. But only if no bus is pulling up (or trying to). If you interfere with an actual bus, you're toast no matter how spryly your passenger hops out.

And while we're on the subject, the definition of a bus zone is not as obvious as it sounds. It's not just the yellow line on the curb, or the length of a normal bus. In fact, it can go on for so long that even a crosswalk can sit in the middle of it – without breaking it up.

The definition of a bus stop zone is this: the whole area from the bus sign down, until either a true corner or another parking sign breaks the zone. This can get unwittingly tricky – like in the case I had where someone brought in pictures of a new sign, including shots of the wet cement, that had been erected after she got the ticket. Her claim was that the ticket should be dismissed because the sign wasn't yet there at the time she was parked there, but ironically, the sign would've actually helped her – by breaking the bus zone, which was her actual violation. In this case, the woman had made two mistakes: She didn't know the definition of a bus stop, and she had thought that she was getting a ticket for the new sign. This just highlights, incidentally, the importance of defending yourself for the right violation: that is, you should always double check your ticket and defense, especially if you have more than one ticket.

Finally, before leaving this section, here's a word or two about commercial loading zones. Only commercial vehicles can stand in "no standing/trucks loading" zones. And, no, it doesn't matter if you're unloading commercial goods; it matters what your license plate is. Passenger vehicles filled to the brim with commercial goods to unload are just plain out of luck here. Including pick-up trucks, vans or SUVs. You're not a "truck" according to the Parking Bureau unless you're displaying commercial plates.

Conversely, just because you're a truck (and you do have the right plates) that doesn't mean that you can unload in *any* "no standing" zone. That's why the City has those special ones. This, by the way, also includes bus tours or charters – if you're unloading like a truck, you can't do it in a regular "no standing" area. About the only exception to this is when it comes to double parking – and for that check out Chapter 20.

So, a harsh section. You can't stand, or hop out leaving your hazards on, or pop open the trunk, or get the fine reduced if you get caught. What else can I tell you? Keep your powder dry and your wits about you, and take what you learned from this section to avoid the next ticket altogether. And may the benign face of fortune smile on you. After all, who knows? Maybe the next ticket will be defective.

## Recap: The Least You Need to Know:

- You're allowed to pick up or drop off passengers in a "no standing" zone, but only if they're not unloading any real bags. And only if you did it in an "expeditious" way.
- Good excuses very rarely work – judges almost never reduce the fine.
- Passenger vehicles can't park in commercial meter zones.
- Unloading in the "trucks loading" zone is only for vehicles with commercial plates.
- Bus stops go all the way to the corner, unless they're broken by another parking sign.
- If you're looking for compassion, go in person. But it's still a long shot.
- Don't forget to read Part 1 – especially about technical defects. With these tickets, they're still your best bet.

# 18. Meters – Expired, Broken, Missing, Overtime

There's nothing more frustrating than racing back to your car to beat the meter and watching from down the road, as a meter maid starts writing out a ticket for your car. Our voices scream out, "wait!" But of course they don't wait. Then we arrive, panting from the exertion, and, gulping for air, we beg them to stop – because we're right here, there's no reason to get the ticket. But of course they don't stop. Some of them even affect not to hear us at all. And at that point, a great surge of rage swells up in our veins and takes over our bodies, and we beat the meter maid to an unrecognizable pulp.

Okay, just kidding about that last. Most likely, we just swallow that rage and then spit it out at the parking ticket judge when he or she is hearing our plea. Although, in the supreme irony section, there was one story circulating in the Parking Bureau about a meter maid who got beaten up and hospitalized only to discover, when she was released, that she had gotten a parking ticket for an expired meter. Veritas, I claimeth not.

So how *does* one go about fighting the injustice of this type of ticket? And, more importantly, how does one *win* the fight?

### Expired Meters

The trouble with the law is that sometimes it just ain't consistent. Remember that I explained, in an earlier section, that the Parking Bureau has an unofficial policy of giving you the first few minutes of a violation off? Well, unfortunately, that policy comes to a screeching stop at the first sign of a meter. One minute over – and most judges will roast you.

It doesn't even matter how great your excuse is. Had a doctor's appointment and the slow-poke kept you overtime? Tough break. Missed the meter because all three of your triplets had to go to the bathroom in the restaurant at the same time? Sorry, honey – no dice (that's a real example, by the way, and the lady even sent in cute pictures of her kids). Couldn't make it back in time because nature called? Next time tell it to call back later – or be prepared to shell out $35–$45 for the privilege of peeing.

Does this seem fair to you?

It didn't seem so to me, either, when I first started working as a judge. And I remember even getting into a whole discussion with a senior judge over the concept of "de minimus non curat lex", which, as I mentioned in chapter sixteen, is the idea that a violation that is very tiny should just be ignored.

Unfortunately, it was a conversation that I lost. Despite my rather vigorous assertion that the principle of de minimus should apply, the consensus among the senior judges was that when it comes to meters even a one minute violation is not tiny. In their view, since meters only run for short times (for example, for a one-hour maximum), each minute really counts.

This, to me, still sounds like a policy begging to be challenged on appeal. I remember one case in particular where a person wrote in that he was busy in the back of his car, fixing the child-seat, when the meter ran out and he got a ticket. Now, it could be that this was a blatant lie, but assuming that it was true, it seems like a perfect example of when the law should blink its raptor eyes and just look the other way. Surely, the time that it takes to buckle a seat ought to be "de minimus"!

So, if you do get into this situation, where you just missed the meter, here's what I suggest: Write or tell the judge that it's a "de minimus" infraction. Point out that a one minute violation of the meter is both financially and time-wise an infinitesimal amount. Financially, each minute at the meter is less than two cents that you've denied the city's coffers. And time-wise, one minute out of twenty-four hours is a joke. As a matter of fact, even taking a one-hour time limit on the meter as being the relevant measure of time to consider, one minute out of sixty is still less than 2 percent of the time. That is, you've gone less than 2 percent overtime on your allotted time limit. Is this not infinitesimal? Has any boss ever paid you any overtime for an extra minute?

Once you get back your "guilty" verdict (which you almost certainly will), you should immediately file an appeal and claim that the judge made a reversible error of law. If that doesn't work, find a lawyer; depending on the circumstances (that is, how angry you are and whether the lawyer is your brother-in-law who will do it for free) it may well be worth fighting it all the way "to the top."

On the other hand, you might want to remember that there is always the possibility that the meter may have been broken.

## Broken Meters

Ask any parking ticket judge, and they'll tell you that at least two thirds of the meters in the city break down on a regular basis. They're constantly breaking, being repaired and breaking down again a day or two later. This being the case, there is a wonderful probability that the meter that zapped you was, in fact, broken.

The City has a procedure for you to follow if you think that the meter was broken. And it consists of making an administrative filing of your claim first. What typically happens next, however, is that the people in charge of answering this claim will look up the repair history for that meter and respond that the meter was not broken *on that day*. You end up getting back a letter telling you that the meter was fine. For most people, the story will end here.

Dear Sir,
   This ticket is unfair. I parked and left. I returned to my car for unknown reason and found the ticket. This left me upset and in mourning for my loss.

What you're not being told, however, is that if you tell the judge that the meter was broken, the judge has the authority to decide that you're right *despite* the record of that particular day. Here's how it works: You claim that the meter wasn't working. The judge then pulls up on his screen the history of that meter. Sure enough, like the administrative section claimed, the meter history shows that the meter was fine that day. But then the judge looks closer. He sees that in the five days on either side of the date of your violation the meter needed to be repaired. It then becomes a reasonable assumption that the meter actually was broken on your day too, but that no one reported it to the City until the next day. And, voilà, your ticket is dismissed.

I'm not urging you to lie here, by the way. There are lots of ways for meters to break down and if you're lying the judge has a fairly good chance of figuring that out. But if you thought that you had an extra two minutes on the meter – maybe you really did.

So, to recap: go through the administrative procedure, get their letter rejecting your claim, ignore it and come on down for a hearing – and walk away (hopefully) happy.

And while we're on the subject of broken meters, here's an example of something *not* to do: If you find yourself at a meter which swallows your coin and doesn't register, don't do what one guy did, and write on the back of a pizza box (that he found on the street, no less) that he paid the meter; sticking the box on his dashboard. Does anyone really expect a cop to be looking that carefully at a windshield?

Instead, find a paper bag and stick it on the meter's head. That way, when the meter maid comes around they can check for themselves that the meter really is broken. And you can avoid the ticket altogether.

Of course, sometimes, you can get the raw end of the stick even when the meter clearly *is* broken when you park there. For instance, I had one case where the person parked at a meter whose head was completely smashed in. Thinking he had caught a break, he parked there with nary a second thought. But by the time he returned to his car, a mere forty-five minutes later, the Department of Transportation had fixed the meter – and he saw a brand-new ticket poking its nose out from under his wipers (never knew the City was that efficient, right?). Fortunately for him, the repair records backed up his claim – and I dismissed the ticket.

But that brings me to my next point. If you *do* park at a broken meter, be careful not to park there for more than sixty minutes. It's the maximum time you get according to the rules.

> Sir:
>
> The meter at which I parked was covered in oil, and was impossible to access. I explained to the officer that no one in their right mind would touch the meter, and he agreed.
>
> Then he handed me the ticket.

## Overtime Parking, Feeding Meters, Muni-meters

The rule when it comes to broken meters is that you get a maximum of one hour to park there. When it comes to missing meters (the meter should be there but it isn't) you get to park there for the maximum limit that the sign on the street says. Thus if the sign says there's a two hour limit for meters, you get two hours. Go beyond those limits, and you risk being slapped with a ticket for "overtime parking."

The important thing to pay attention to here is not to inadvertently admit to guilt. For example, I had one case where a very irate defendant claimed that he was parked in a spot for four hours, feeding the meter every hour, before the meter broke down – and he got a ticket for overtime parking. His claim was that the meter broke, and therefore he shouldn't have to pay – but he was only allowed at that meter for a maximum of one hour according to the posted signs. Sheesh!

In case you don't know (and I didn't, before I became a judge), if you feed the meter and overstay your limit, you absolutely can get a ticket – for overtime parking. And if the cop sees you feeding the meter, the violation will be "feeding meter." This, by the way, is why it's important to notice what it is the signs actually say. The signs tell you not just how long the meters allow you to park there, but also when you are allowed to use them.

They also sometimes tell you to use a Muni meter machine. And if you did, and still got a ticket – don't fret. Just send in your receipt and all will be dismissed. Although you might want to be careful about where you get that receipt. The rule is: You must get the Muni meter receipt from somewhere close to where you parked (the machines have numbers, so their location can be checked, even though in practice they often aren't). This was reiterated to us at one point when one big company with many vehicles decided to be "smart" and pool all of their receipts, sending them in as defenses if the time was correct. What they did, though, was alert the Parking Bureau to fraud – since it's highly unlikely that a driver in Brooklyn bought a spot from a machine in Queens!

Oops.

## Technical Defects

Finally, some technical things to look out for on meter-related tickets. First, make sure that the meter's number is on the ticket. If it's missing in action – your ticket will be dismissed.

And if you get hit with overtime parking, check to see if the officer remembered to include the "time first observed," as he must. If it's not there, you get off free. Similarly, if the "days in effect" or "hours in effect" is screwed up – free again. Generally, these are good places to look for classic careless mistakes by the police. Another one? Forgetting to check off "AM" or "PM" for the time.

And while we're on the subject of time, if the meter is broken or missing, then the effective time limit should be written on the ticket. That is, however long you're allowed to park there should be stated.

Furthermore, you should probably also look for the place on the ticket where it says if the meter is operational. I had one case – on an electronic ticket, no less – where the violation was for overtime at a broken meter. But the ticket itself had the box checked off that the meter was operational – a prima facie contradiction. Goodbye ticket and hello lucky for someone that I caught that.

And, finally, smile. If all the above fails to help you, look at it this way: no matter how bad things get, they could be worse – the ticket could have been for a pedestrian ramp (a whopping $185). Right?

### Recap: The Least You Need to Know:

- If you only just missed the meter, try the "de minimus" defense.
- Double check your watch. If the meter is fast, it's probably broken.
- You get sixty minutes at a broken meter and up to the time limit posted on the sign in the street if the meter is missing altogether.

- Always gets the Muni meter receipt from close to where you parked.
- Always check for technical defects related to meters, especially "AM/PM" mistakes.

## 19. Fire Hydrants

You can't learn how to drive without learning the rules, yet somewhere along the line most of us manage to forget at least some of the details. And the classic example of this is the rule about how many feet you have to allow between your car and a fire hydrant. By the time I applied to become a parking ticket judge I had been driving for at least a decade and a half and if anyone had asked me about how much space I should give a hydrant, I probably would've shrugged and said, "who knows? Enough that a fire truck can get to it."

So it didn't surprise me a bit when we learned, during training, that literally thousands of people defend their fire hydrant tickets by inadvertently shooting themselves right in the wallet. The way it works is like this: A respondent comes in for a hearing, face red with indignity, clutching the ticket like a warrior holding a spear and sits down with a huff, opposite the judge. "This ticket says I was eight feet from the hydrant," he or she would charge, "but I wasn't! I was a full ten feet away! Ten feet!" And the judge grimaces briefly, nods at the respondent and says quietly, "I believe you. I'm sure that you were ten feet away. The problem is that the law says fifteen feet." And another guilty verdict is born.

This is an easy mistake to avoid. There aren't many numbers that you need to know when driving – so remember the number fifteen. And if you're in Manhattan, there is an easy rule of thumb to guide you: fifteen feet is roughly the length of three sidewalk squares. Judges know this, so you're far better off saying that you were three squares away from the hydrant than saying, for example, that you paced the distance, and according to your shoe size, you were sixteen feet from the hydrant. This actually happens all the time. People claim to have measured the distance accurately – and they tell some of the strangest stories judges get to hear.

For example, one man actually sent in a picture of his shoe; supposedly to show that fifteen paces (foot over foot) equaled fifteen feet. Of course, he forgot that he still has to be believable that he paced it out that day and that the cop got it wrong. Which, let's face it, is a difficult burden to overcome.

And it doesn't help your case much to claim that you never received the ticket and only found out about it online much later, but still, you remember that you paced out the distance accurately that very day. Now I ask you: Would *you* believe you in that case?

> How come they don't give tickets out to the people who really deserve them? Why must they pick on me?
>
> – An irate driver overheard on the street

On par with that example are the defenses that claim that there was enough room and show us a picture of where the car was parked. But how, I ask you, are we to know that you didn't simply move your car back a few feet after getting the ticket, but before snapping the picture? Although perhaps if you make a habit of doing this every time you're near a hydrant and do it, say, with your cell phone, and if your phone automatically records the time, then I'd say that you have at least a good shot at getting the ticket dismissed. That is, *if* your picture shows us that you truly *did* park far enough away from the hydrant before the ticket was issued.

Incidentally, humor will sometimes help you here. There was one case that the judge sitting next to me received that we all got a kick out of. A young girl, trying to show how far away the car was from the hydrant, sent in a picture of two people where one of the people was grabbing the hydrant while balancing on one foot, and had stretched herself out like a star. Meanwhile, the second person, also balanced and stretched out like a star had grabbed the first girl's outstretched leg with her hand, and with her dangling foot just barely touched the parked car. The judge who saw this just cracked up and said "I have to dismiss this – I don't care what they say."

But generally, you need to know that the magic number is fifteen and that no evidence about yellow lines (or lack thereof) really matters. At the risk of beating a dead dog, let me stress that the City doesn't owe drivers any yellow lines or other indicators of where the zone ends. And in any case, the lines are sometimes wrong, even where they do exist.

Similarly, asking a passing cop or other people or just "doing your best" usually won't impress most judges. (Although I must admit that I did feel a passing wave of sympathy for the respondent who wrote that "I'm

82, and I should know by now how far I was from the hydrant.")

So what should you do if you get a hydrant ticket? First, check it for defects. In addition to the usual ones (see Chapter 1), make sure that the cop wrote in the actual number of feet that you were away from the hydrant (and, yes, zero is a number). If he forgot this detail, you walk free. Unfortunately, though, don't bother writing in that he didn't put down the number of inches – by law, he doesn't have to.

Secondly, try to avoid excuses that sound very unlikely – even if they are completely true. Explanations like "another car must have pushed my car closer to the hydrant by bumping me." I actually groaned out loud when I heard that one.

Thirdly, if you're going to try for a defense that relies on your credibility about how far away you were from the hydrant, come in for a live hearing. It just stands to reason that you have a better shot convincing the judge that you're telling the truth if you're right there before her and answering any questions that she might have. Besides, some judges really don't like trouble (and by trouble they mean arguing with respondents, especially super-sized ones). Or, as one of my colleagues once said to me, "if it's live, and they're only five feet from the hydrant – no problem."

Finally, there are a few more things that you need to know that could help you out. One is that you can get a ticket even for parking next to a broken hydrant. I had a case once where the hydrant was so broken that you could see clear through it to the other side – it looked like it had been blasted straight through by a shotgun. But it was still no dice when it came to the verdict – because, theoretically at least, the Fire Department could still fix it if they needed it that day. That was a tough one for me to accept at first; I had already written out a judgment dismissing the ticket when a senior judge told me that she had asked the other seniors and the consensus was to find him guilty. I wanted to at least reduce the fine, but a hydrant is a "no stopping" area and policy is not to reduce. The lesson from this? If you're going to claim that the hydrant doesn't work, go to the nearest Fire Department first. Get a letter from them that states clearly that the hydrant is no longer in use, and *then* come in to defend your ticket.

The next thing you need to know is that the City frowns on disabled vehicles being parked at a hydrant. So unless you were there legally when you broke down – don't push your car to the hydrant. It's actually better to leave it double parked. But how, you may ask, could you be there legally to begin with? The answer to that question brings us to the last but most important thing to know about fire hydrant tickets: The absolutely best defense for a hydrant ticket is one that almost no one is aware of. It's called the "daylight exception" rule.

The daylight exception rule is that if you're driving a passenger vehicle during daylight hours (defined legally for this rule as being from sunrise to sunset), and the driver remains sitting behind the wheel, you can go right ahead and park next to that hydrant for just as long as you like (well, at least until someone from the Fire Department comes by to use it, anyway). Taxi drivers have it even better; they get to use this exception and sit next to fire hydrants even at night. This is an amazing rule, and something of a ridiculous one, but it's on the statute books and there to be used and enjoyed by all of us. The only exception to it is that standing can't be otherwise prohibited, such as by another "no standing" sign that overlaps the hydrant zone. Ain't that one amazing? Be sure to use it at a live hearing – and watch the judge's eyes pop.

### Recap: The Least You Need to Know:

- The rule is that you can't park within fifteen feet of a hydrant.
- The number of feet away must be on the ticket; if it's missing then the ticket is defective.
- If your credibility is on the line about how far away you were – go for a live hearing.
- You can get a ticket even for a broken hydrant.
- Use the "daylight exception" rule, if it applies.

## 20. Double Parking & Traffic Lanes

It happens every morning. The alarm rings, and it's an unholy early morning. You glance at the clock and convince yourself that it's okay; you really have plenty of time. So you hit the snooze. Then you hit it again. And then – you're suddenly smack in the middle of a race to move your car before you get a ticket for street cleaning.

Every New Yorker knows what comes next. If you're lucky, your mad dash to the street succeeds and you get to your car in time and drive it just across the road, double parking it to wait out the street cleaning. And local lore has it that as long as you're sitting in the car, no cop can give you a ticket.

But local lore is dead wrong. And believe it or not, all of those cops driving around *not* giving out tickets should get your eternal gratitude (or at least a really nice Christmas gift), because legally they could slap a ticket on every double parked car they find, whether someone is in it or not. And be finished their quota by ten o'clock in the morning.

Yes, folks, it's true. Double parking really is *that* illegal. And what's worse, it's really very difficult to squirm

139

your way out of the charge. Believe me, I know. I've had too many cases where people complained about everything from the difficulty in *not* double parking to lawyers citing Supreme Court case law about "selective prosecution," and how it's illegal for cops to ticket *their* car when the guy next to them got off scot-free.

None of it works. Okay, I did hear of one case (count it – one), where someone used the "selective prosecution" defense successfully. But it was a person whose neighbor was a cop and he could prove that the cop gave him the ticket as part of a harassment campaign to get him to move a fence or some other shared-property silliness. If it's a random cop giving out tickets – save your breath.

So, if you can't just scream "unfair!" then what can you do?

For starters, try all the general defenses in Part 1. But then you knew that. So when you're done with those options, realize that the reason that double parking is such a hard ticket to escape is that it's really a "no standing" violation. And as a "no standing" violation, it's subject to the same stringent rules – which means, among other things, that the judges are strongly discouraged from reducing the fine.

But there is good news, too. Since double parking is technically just another type of "no standing" zone, you *are* allowed to double park in order to drop off or pick up passengers, same as in every

> To Whom It May Concern:
>
> When I got this ticket I was livid, to say the least. I had not parked illegally. I checked and double-checked. Then I drove to the police precinct and was told by the officers there that it's the end of the month and quotas have to be met. I couldn't believe this was happening in a democracy. If that's what we are still.
>
> You must dismiss this ticket.

other "no standing" zone. Just remember not to open the trunk, though; it's passengers only, not their bags.

This isn't as obvious as it may seem. If you are arguing in front of a judge (or by mail) that you were stopping just long enough to pick someone up or drop them off, you'd be well advised to point out that you know that the law allows you to do this. That way, if they wrongfully convict you, you'll have something to say on appeal. Unfortunately, there are too many judges that have forgotten this rule and just say "guilty" as soon as they hear the words "double park".

In fact, in my first week on the job I dismissed a ticket for that very reason, and a senior judge gave me hell for it. When I pointed out that the law was written that way, she flat out contradicted me. It took me fifteen minutes and the support of two other senior judges to convince her that she had been wrong about the rules for double parking – for years. When she did finally concede the point, you know what she said? She declared, "I've found hundreds of people guilty, and I've never once been reversed on appeal."

And it wouldn't surprise me a bit if when she gets a double parking case today, she still reflexively says "guilty."

So, know your rights. It's the first step.

The second step is to know when you're wrong.

There are a few common misconceptions about double parking, and I know that I was guilty of thinking them, too, before I became a judge. The most common is that if you leave the engine running, or the hazard lights on, or you leave a passenger in the car, that it's okay to double park.

Nope. Sorry. No dice. We must get hundreds of

defenses like these every day, and none of them work. I'm not sure how this particular piece of urban mythology started, but it isn't doing anybody any favors. Although I must admit that possibly my all-time favorite defense of any parking ticket that I ever adjudicated, was the letter that I got claiming that "I double parked, but it was okay, because *I left my dog in the car*(!!)." Honestly, I can't make this stuff up.

Also a no-go if you're driving a passenger vehicle: The defense that you double parked just "to quickly load something that I bought." If you're driving a commercial vehicle, see below. But if not, once again, that's a "no standing" violation. Which means that you can drop off or pick up *people*, not bags.

To be fair, there may be some flexibility to this rule, though – as long as it's reasonable. For instance, if the person you're dropping off is disabled and their wheelchair or crutches are in the back, you can make a good argument (and I've accepted this myself) that the crutches or wheelchair are really a "part of" the person that you're dropping off. And, therefore, getting them out of the car is perfectly legit.

Although one can certainly take this too far. Like in the case of the lady who claimed that she was disabled because of a temporary cast on her leg – and then went on to describe how she got out of her van to help her nephews load up their suitcases. All while being double parked on Broadway. This character had the audacity to threaten to "sue the city" if we didn't dismiss her ticket. Needless to say, her threat didn't exactly send shivers down our spines.

So, to sum up: If you're driving a passenger vehicle, double parking is precarious. Use the general defenses and the "no standing" defenses, and if you're arguing that you were just dropping someone off, I'd advise you to take that person with you and argue it at a live hearing.

## Double Parking vs. Traffic Lanes

In case you're wondering, if you get a ticket for a "traffic lane" violation, that means almost the same as double parking. The major difference is that with traffic lane tickets, the cop is saying that there was room to park at the side of the curb. Double parking, on the other hand, means there was a car at the curb already.

This is only important if you can prove that there actually *was* a car there, in which case the traffic lane ticket is incorrect – and you get off scot-free. Credibility being the issue here, any pictures or witnesses will help.

There's also one more thing to note about a traffic lane violation: It's technically a "no stopping" zone, which means that you can't even off-load or pick up any passengers, no matter how quickly you do it. This is in distinct contrast to double parking, which is a "no standing" zone. Cabbies beware.

## Double parking & Commercial Vehicles

If you drive a commercial vehicle, you're probably already aware of this one perk: Outside of midtown Manhattan, you are allowed to double park almost any-where. There *are* a few rules, though, that you need to be aware of, (for the legal minded amongst you, check out section 4–08(f)(1) of the NYC Traffic Rules).

First off, remember that the burden of proof is on *you*. While it's true that you can get a "get-out-of-jail-free" card for both double parking and traffic lane violations, that's only if you can prove that you were there doing "expeditious commercial activity" (This is also true for "no standing/trucks loading" zones).

What that means is that you were loading/unloading as quickly and efficiently as possible under the circumstances.

How to prove this? First off, *don't* just send in your invoice. I can't tell you how many times a company sent in an invoice and nothing else and expected us to (a) decipher it and (b) decode from it that the work was done expeditiously. The only thing that an invoice like that tells us is that you have access to invoice stationary.

What you really need is a story – from the driver. The best thing, in fact, would be a formal affidavit from the driver (notarized and everything), telling us exactly what happened and how long he was there and why it took so long. But even if it's not an affidavit, at least let him write in with some of the details! What was it that he was loading? Why should we ignore the cop's note on the ticket that claims the van was there for forty-five minutes?

Incidentally, this is especially important if your ticket hails from a location near your place of business. It doesn't take a genius to figure out that it's less believable that you were parked there only for "expeditious loading" when your store-front is right down the street. Spin a yarn. Play Scheherazade. Make us believe you.

And one last thing: even though you're allowed to double park, remember that there can't be curb-side space available within one hundred feet of your truck. Don't get caught letting the little things trip you up.

## Recap: The Least You Need to Know:

- Double parking is a "no standing" violation.
- Picking up/letting off passengers is still allowed.
- Leaving someone in the car does not help you.
- If there was space available at the curb, it's a traffic lane ticket.
- Commercial vehicles still need to prove expeditious commercial activity. Tell us a story.

# 21. Crosswalks & Pedestrian Ramps

You wouldn't normally think that there was much to argue about if you got a ticket for stopping, standing or parking in a crosswalk. But there *are* a few rules to know that can help you out.

To start with, don't waste your breath arguing that there were no lines on the street marking the crosswalk. According to the law, they don't need to mark them. Also, don't bother with the excuse that only the nose of your car was in the zone. As far as the Parking Bureau cares, that nose is big enough to count as the whole animal. That one I know from personal experience – I got zapped by it once myself, before I became a judge.

Similarly, even the "de minimus" argument that I've urged in other parts of this book isn't likely to help you here, because a crosswalk is a "no stopping" zone. And as you probably know by now, the rules for "no stopping" zones are the strictest ones around.

So what exactly *can* you do?

Well, first of all, you can know the definition of a crosswalk, so that if you want to argue that you weren't really parked in it you'll sound far more believable. You might think that this is obvious, but you'd be surprised at how many people diligently describe exactly where they were parked, in an attempt to prove their case – and end up proving the prosecution's case for them. Because they don't know what a crosswalk really is.

The definition of a crosswalk is the following: "that part of a roadway, whether marked or unmarked, which is included within the extensions of the sidewalk lines between opposite sides of the roadway at an intersection" (Section 4–01 of the NYC Traffic Rules). Sounds a bit like gibberish, doesn't it? The important part here is the "extensions of the sidewalk lines." Basically, that means that you need to look at where the buildings end and the sidewalks begin and then draw an imaginary line across the street. Anything on the side of the line that *doesn't* include buildings and does include sidewalks and roads is a crosswalk. Then persuade the judge that you weren't really parked there.

The next thing to know is that this is, I stress, a "no stopping" zone (okay, I'm repeating myself, but it's that important). That means that if your defense starts with "I just stopped for a minute to let someone out of the car" (pay attention, cabbies!), you've just shot yourself in the foot. Outside of all the defenses listed in Part I, there's little hope in convincing a judge that you were right to have stopped there.

Otherwise, there's only one more thing (besides looking for technical defects, of course) left to do: Count yourself lucky that they didn't hit you with a "pedestrian ramp" ticket too.

### Pedestrian Ramps

Pedestrian ramps are probably the sneakiest tickets around. Most people don't even know what pedestrian ramps are. So here's a quick definition: they're the part of the curb that is lowered to help the disabled. And when they're not hanging out in the middle of a crosswalk, they're notoriously easy to miss. To add insult to injury, they're the most expensive tickets you're ever likely to get. Clocking in, to date, at a whopping $185.

So what do you do if you get one?

The world of pedestrian ramps can be divided in two: Those found at crosswalks and those found in the middle of the street. The ramps at crosswalks are killer-tickets. Since a pedestrian ramp violation is technically a wholly separate violation, if a cop wants to be mean he can charge you with both a crosswalk violation *and* a pedestrian ramp violation (technically, a pedestrian ramp is a "no standing" zone, so you can drop off or pick up passengers next to one – but not their luggage – but that won't help you in a crosswalk). But it's the ones in the middle of the street that usually give people ulcers. They're particularly easy to miss because they're so unpredictable; there are plenty of streets without them and plenty with – yet no external signpost warns you that they're there.

So far as I know there's only one effective way of fighting these tickets: You have to be able to credibly prove that you had no notice that the ramp was there. That is, you have to prove you couldn't and didn't see it.

Now, usually ignorance is a terrible defense in the law world. But in this case it works, because (for due process reasons) if you had no notice that the ramp was there, you couldn't possibly be expected to adhere to the rules governing it. And the ticket must be dismissed.

Generally, pictures help. But they are not technically needed. Let's say that it snowed the day before the ticket was issued and the snow covered the curb, preventing you from seeing the pedestrian ramp. That's a good example of a phenomenon that every judge is familiar with. Especially if the ticket was given at night, when naturally it's harder to see. In this case you may not even need a picture to prove your case (still, it sure can't hurt). Personally, I dismissed many snow-covered ramp tickets and was more than happy to do it. Then again, I know of one judge who would never believe snow excuses without explicit pictures.

Other examples? There was one case where someone sent in a picture of a homeowner's overflowing garbage bags that clearly deluged the ramp. In another instance it was a pile-up of old furniture. In both cases, I was willing to believe the driver's innocence.

Following far behind, the other possible defense that you can try is denial: You were really parked further away. Unfortunately, like most general denials, you probably won't be believed. But if you want to strengthen your case, pay close attention to the exact address on the ticket. If the ramp is not directly in front of that location – you're in luck.

Incidentally, pictures of your car parked near the ramp (but not next to it) probably won't help. Unless there's a time-stamp on the photo (and preferably from something difficult to forge) and the time is literally the same as that printed on the ticket, most judges will just assume that you moved your car before snapping the shot. Sorry.

So remember, the best defense here is an effective case of ignorance. Hey, sometimes it really is bliss.

**Recap: The Least You Need to Know:**

- Crosswalks are "no stopping" zones, so don't drop off/pick up passengers.
- When defending a ticket, remember to *define* a crosswalk first, and then show that you weren't in one.
- Pedestrian ramps are "no standing" zones.
- The ramps don't need a sign to tell you that they are there.
- The best defense for a pedestrian ramp is to prove that you couldn't have known that it was there.

# 22. Obstructing a Driveway

As a sometime resident of suburbia, I can identify all too well with the judge who once remarked to me "I hate people who block driveways. It's the worst violation. It pisses me off. There is a special place in hell just for those people."

If you haven't had the agony of this happening to you, let me paint you a picture. You wake up in the morning, in a rush, needing to be somewhere by 9 AM. You've made the trip hundreds of times so you know just how long it'll take you once you're behind the wheel. Only, when you get to your car, you realize that you're going nowhere. Your evil neighbor has parked their car in a way calculated to block your exit. You holler in frustration, you honk your horn and finally you call the police. And if you're lucky, they actually arrive and tow the offending vehicle away. But only if you're lucky.

So why, you might ask, am I including a section on how to get out of these tickets?

Because sometimes it's the good guys who get hit with 'em. For example, I adjudicated one case where a lady had the upsetting experience that I described above, and she called the police. And they came. Only they arrived *five hours later*. By that time the offending car was long gone, her own car was blocking her own driveway – and she got a ticket.

Alternatively, you could be in the position of the man who got a "driveway" ticket when there *was* no driveway. Except for the one two doors down.

So how do you fight these? Simply. If there wasn't any driveway, you need to take pictures – lots of 'em. The whole street, in fact. The goal is to show us the signs as well as whatever address is on the ticket, to show a lack of a driveway. And it would help if there was a meter nearby, to show that even the City realizes that it's a parking spot (rather than a driveway).

If it's your own driveway – just say so and bring in (or send in a copy) of your registration. If your car is registered to the address on the ticket, you'll get the ticket dismissed. If, by the way, you just moved in, get the registration changed *first* and then send it in, perhaps with a copy of your lease. If nothing else, it shows good faith (which, at the least, ought to give you a reduction of the fine, assuming that they don't hammer you for any delays in getting the registration fixed).

And if it happens that you're *not* one of the good guys – play nice, okay? That special section of hell is full enough already.

### Recap: The Least You Need to Know:

- If your car is registered to that address, you will get the ticket dismissed.
- If your claim is that the driveway isn't there or wasn't blocked – send in lots of pictures.

# 23. Status Violations – Equipment, Registration, License Plates, Inspection.

You can get a parking ticket that has nothing to do with how you parked. When you do, these are called "status violations" and the main "benefit" of getting one is that if you get more than one on the same day, only one will count. If you get more than one in a week, all the others will be reduced to $20 each.

Status violations are tickets for something that's wrong with your car, not its location, and the main ones are for missing equipment, registration or inspection stickers that are somehow improper, and license plates that are awry.

Here's what to do if you get one:

### Missing equipment
Section 4–08(n)(8) of the NYC Traffic Rules mandates that vehicles must have proper equipment, and there's nothing to be gained by trying to defend a broken tail light or missing driver-side mirror by explaining how you don't really need one.

Instead, just do two things: First, make sure that the ticket tells you exactly what is missing – if it doesn't, the ticket's defective. Then, just fix the problem within twenty-four hours.

For law buffs:

VTL Section 376(a) also comes into play. It states: "it shall be unlawful to...operate, drive or park a vehicle...during the period from one-half hour after sunset to one-half hour before sunrise, unless such vehicle is equipped with lamps...in good working condition."

When you're done, go to the Parking Bureau with a receipt that shows that you fixed the problem within a day (or send it in by mail) and the summons will be dismissed. Easy as apple pie. Although personally I find apple pie kind of annoying; but that's another story.

## Registration

New York State vehicles need to be registered and the sticker needs to be current. Every year thousands of people get hit with "expired registration" tickets, and as long as the cop wrote the expiration date somewhere on the ticket, the ticket is valid. Assuming that your registration really has expired, there's not much for you to do except fix it and avoid another ticket.

But what if you just screwed up on the sticker? You registered the vehicle on time, and forgot to paste the update on the car. Or, as in one case that I received, you have two cars – and you accidentally mixed up the stickers, so that now both cars are displaying the wrong one. Is there a way out of the ticket?

Technically, no. Since it's a status problem, the fact that your behavior was angelic doesn't excuse the violation. Although almost all judges will at least reduce the fine if they believe you. But if you insist on trying to get out of the whole fine, here's a case where I'd advise you to fight in person. No matter what people may think, judges are human, and dislike giving guilty verdicts when they seem unfair. At least not to the defendant's face, anyway. I've known judges who will search hard for any technical defects in these kinds of cases. Very hard.

And here are some defects you should look for in any "registration" ticket: First, make sure that the expiration date appears on your ticket. Second, if the ticket is for an "improper" display or an "improper" registration, make sure that the cop wrote in exactly *how* it was improper. For example, a van which needs "com" registration but has "pas" instead is improper –

> To the Judge:
> So my sticker expired. I just forgot to check the date, that's all. I replaced it yesterday. Now please dismiss the ticket. As it is, the violation is asinine. Who cares what the sticker says, as long as the car is registered?

but if a cop just writes "should be com," that isn't sufficient. The cop needs to write *why* it should be "com". For example, he needs to write "no rear side window," which shows a lack of something that every "pas" vehicle needs.

Sometimes it looks as though the cop screwed up by not putting down the expiration date, but he didn't. For instance, if the date is missing, and he wrote in "N/S" ("Not Shown"). Or if the ticket says "snow covering registration" (which explains why he didn't list it). Although, I have known people to get lucky with that one. For instance, one judge told me that she always dismisses snow-covered excuses. "The cops are being lazy," she said. "They just never got out of their car – so I dismiss these."

If the ticket is for a mismatched plate/sticker, that means the physical license plate is different than the one shown in the registration sticker. This happens most often when you just bought the car, but it is also one of the classic frauds used to try to get out of tickets (by people assuming the plate will be 'wrong' on their ticket). Since the Parking Bureau takes a dim view of this, the only thing to do is to check carefully to see if both the registered plate information and the alternate plate information are written down on the summons. If the ticket is missing something (for example, the physical plate's State information) then the ticket will be dismissed.

> **A Partial List of Plate Types:**
>
> PAS – Passenger or suburban cars
>
> COM – Commercial
>
> IRP – International Registration Plan
>
> SRF – Special Passenger
>
> DLR – Dealer
>
> NYS – New York Senate
>
> MED – Medical Doctor
>
> OML – Omnibus, Livery
>
> AMB – Ambulance

### Missing Plate/Improper Display

If your vehicle is from out of New York State, you only need a rear plate. Otherwise, you need both. And they both need to be "properly" attached. If the cop checks off the "improper" box, make sure he explains *how* it's improper and which plate it is (for example, "front plate on dash"). If he doesn't, you get this one for free.

### Inspection [NYS Vehicles Only]

Similar to registration, if you get a ticket for an expired inspection sticker, the expiration date must be somewhere on the face of the summons. If it isn't – it's a free pass. And also similar to registration, excuses as to why the period expired without you renewing it are generally ineffective.

Here are a few excuses that we hear all the time and that *won't* get sympathy: "I had no time to get it inspected"; "I was out of town"; "I went on that date but they couldn't do it in time", and "I got it done the very next day."

> Sir/Madam:
> This ticket is incorrect. Please invite the officer to come to Court and clarify so that she might learn something.

Better excuses tend to be medical emergencies, and "I was in the Army just then." And even these don't guarantee you anything without some serious paperwork documenting your inability to get it done on time.

And one last note about common excuses. If your excuse is that it was your kid's responsibility to take care of it, you will get sympathy, at least from the older judges. Unfortunately, they'll also tell you that it's still your name on the ownership and force you to ante up. Still, it may be your only card to play, and if you're lucky, a judge whose teenager is driving him crazy at home will at least reduce the fine. Hey, you never know. (And this is the kind of excuse that will probably work better at a live hearing).

Also similar to registration, if the ticket is for an "improper display" of the inspection sticker, the officer needs to say *how* it was improper. If he doesn't spell it out – you get off free.

Incidentally, since inspection violations only apply to New York State vehicles, what happens if you just moved to New York? Or you bought the car out of state?

If you were a non-resident of New York and became a resident, the law allows your out-of-state inspection to be valid until it expires, or for one year from the date of being registered in New York. Whichever is sooner. Just send in all the paperwork and rest easy.

If you are a resident of New York but bought (or got as a gift or otherwise acquired), a car in, say, New Jersey, then when you register it in New York you'll get a ten day grace period (with a temporary sticker) to get the car inspected in New York. Don't forget to *use* the sticker. And try not to mention that it took you ten months to register your car to begin with, since technically that's also illegal and can't do you any good to admit.

### Recap: The Least You Need to Know:

- For repeat tickets: Same-day tickets will be dismissed; within one week, the second (and third and fourth...) will be reduced to $20 each.
- Fix missing equipment tickets within twenty-four hours, and they'll be dismissed.
- Check for technical defects: expiration date, the reason why it's "improper" and the rest.
- Excuses for missing the deadline for expired stickers rarely work unless you were genuinely and actually incapable of getting it done on time.
- If you have a great excuse, you're better off fighting the ticket in person.

# PART III

## BEYOND THE DEFENSE:
### *The Rest of the Story*

## 24. Guilty with an Excuse – When to Throw Yourself on the Mercy of the Court – and When Not to Bother

Sometimes the cops get it right. You *were* parked illegally. The ticket *isn't* defective or illegible. It *wasn't* your day. So what do you do? Do you throw in the towel and just pay up?

Personally, I think it's always advisable to at least ask the judges (by mail or through the web) to look for defects. If you do this online, the process takes only a few minutes and the judge will only see the official ticket, which may have been scanned in badly and be illegible, officially – to your great benefit.

But there are times when what's really bothering us is that although we *were* parked illegally, we only did it because we had a really good reason. *Anyone* would have done the same thing. And we're convinced that if we tell the judge our excuse he'll have no choice but to dismiss the whole thing. Or at least reduce the fine.

If that's the case for you, then read on and find out what to expect – and how to avoid some common pitfalls.

> I believe in getting into hot water; it keeps you clean.
>
> – G.K. Chesterton

### The Law

The law allows judges to reduce fines and penalties. Specifically, the Commissioner's Rules (Title 34 of the Rules of the City of New York, Section 39–05(2)(c)) says: "upon a showing of good cause made by the respondent...any scheduled fine may be reduced. The Director may fix the procedure for such reduction."

That being the case, the question is what exactly is "good cause?" And the answer is a little like that famous quote about pornography: I can't define it, but I know it when I see it. More generally, good cause means some unusual circumstances, a limited violation of the law and some respect for that nebulous idea of "in the public interest."

And, so, although I can't define "good cause" precisely, I *can* give you examples of what it is and what it isn't.

Let's say you got a ticket for parking your car somewhere in a "no parking" zone that only comes into effect on Tuesdays. And let's say that you were out of the state the previous weekend, with your return ticket scheduled for Monday night. But then you got delayed, through no fault of your own, and by the time you got to your car on Tuesday afternoon, you have a ticket. This would be a perfect example of what the Parking Bureau calls "Absence from Jurisdiction." And it ought to earn you a reduction of the fine. Of course, in a perfect world it would earn you a get-out-of-this-ticket free card, but the Parking Bureau just calls it a good excuse to reduce.

Or let's say that you were in the hospital at the time, or a fire or flood destroyed all the records in your office – and, of course, you paid the summons in as timely a way as possible under the circumstances – but still late. These clearly, are good excuses, and your late fine(s) should be erased.

Similarly, if you never got the original ticket. This is surely a good reason for the judge to at least knock off the $10 penalty for not answering it. Or if you did send in the ticket and the Parking Bureau somehow lost it.

If you're noticing, all of the above examples have something in common: A lack of will or intent, on your part, to do something unlawful. As a rule, these are the best kinds of excuses.

But they're not the only kind. I've reduced fines for people who made genuine efforts to avoid being in the wrong or tried, as best as they could, to at least have their car commit as minimal a violation as possible. For example, if we believe you that only the tail bumper of your car was in the forbidden zone, you could get a reduction for "half in prohibited zone."

Part of the key to this, of course, is to work on our sympathy. Force us to identify with you in your situation. In practice, this often means that the best way to get a reduction is to come down and ask for it in person. It's simply too easy for us to be indifferent towards a piece of paper. On the other hand, no matter how hardhearted a judge is, a plea for compassion has a fighting chance when the judge sees the tears in your eyes.

And while you're down there, be sure to throw in (if it's true) that you submitted your defense in as timely a way as possible and that you have a record of good faith compliance with paying tickets in the past. Both of these are, officially, "good causes" to mitigate a fine – but when sent in by mail they are routinely overlooked by judges as being irrelevant.

## Bad Excuses

All that being said, here are a few excuses to avoid, if at all possible:

"I had no time to come down." This shouldn't surprise people, but it often does: The Parking Bureau does not care about how busy you are. Their logic goes basically like this: Everyone is busy. New York City, in particular, is one of the busiest places on the globe. So being too busy is just par for the course. As one senior judge explained it, "if you're too busy to mail in the defense, you should be that much more careful about committing the offense." Do not expect more than passing sympathy for this one.

"The ticket was unfair." Well, obviously, you feel that way. You may even be right. The sign probably *shouldn't* be on that corner when it makes so much more sense for it to be on the next street. And clearly that cop had something against you by writing you the ticket, even though he saw you running frantically down the street.

It isn't as though we don't care that you got zapped with a ticket; it's that writing down "fine reduced because respondent was late arriving at the meter" does not sound like a "good cause", legally. Remember, the circumstances that you're arguing are supposed to be *unusual.* Perhaps if you were hobbling towards that meter with a cane, or crutches. In any case, although you might have some success with this approach (in person), I recommend against it.

"My employee screwed up and didn't pay it on time." This one ought to work, if life was completely fair. But legally you are still on the hook despite your worker's incompetence. On the bright side, you may be able to take the money out of the poor guy's paycheck – or just make his life miserable for a few days as petty revenge.

And, finally, the mother of all bad excuses: "I have no money."

This is probably the most ubiquitous complaint and it generally starts off with someone saying "I'm a baby-sitter and can barely afford the gas," or "I'm a teacher working for coolie wages," or "I'm a student", or on welfare, unemployed, in retirement, thinking about retirement, thinking about becoming unemployed…you get the picture.

What they all have in common is that we believe every one of them. The parking ticket fines *are* exorbitant. Living in New York *is* expensive enough. Money *doesn't* grow on trees. The trouble is that the Parking Bureau's attitude is that if you can't afford to pay the fine, you shouldn't be driving. Basically, the City feels that the public transport system is great. And if you're too poor to pay the fine, ride the subway (not very compassionate, are they?).

> I'm living so far beyond my income that we may almost be said to be living apart.
>
> – ee cummings

There *are* extreme cases where a plea of "personal

hardship" will help you reduce the fine. But by definition, they must be quite unusual – and for the most part
they won't revolve around Mammon. Think close rela-
tives, injured severely in a tornado, forcing you to catch
the next flight out to take care of them. That's the kind
of hardship the Parking Bureau is looking for.

But no matter what your excuse, "good cause" or
not, there are a few kinds of tickets where it generally
doesn't even pay to bother trying.

### When Success is Very Unlikely

Notwithstanding the fact that *officially* the law doesn't
discriminate as to when a judge has the authority to
mitigate a fine and when he doesn't, there are some
tickets that are on the Parking Bureau's "no way" list,
unless fire, famine and plague all hit New York City si-
multaneously. These are tickets for handicapped zones,
"no stopping" zones and "no standing" zones.

When you think about it, that's a lot of tickets. "No
stopping" includes fire hydrants, traffic lanes, bike lanes,
crosswalks and intersections. And "no standing" includes double parking. What this means in practice is
that if you have a ticket in one of those categories, and
you really can't afford to pay for it, you absolutely must
plead for it in person – because you really are fighting
City Hall. And you'd better come armed with an absolutely amazing excuse – one that exonerates you completely from fault. Because dollars to doughnuts, it ain't
likely that you'll come out of there happy.

### The Amount That Will Be Mitigated

The last thing that you need to know is to temper your
expectations when it comes to getting the fine reduced.

It used to be the case (and with some of the older judges, in live hearings, it still is) that the judge would reduce the amount of the ticket completely according to his or her own discretion. The result was a wildly arbitrary system, where two people with identical tickets and excuses could walk out with two different fines – one person having had a fine reduced by $5 and the other having had his fine reduced *to* $5.

In response, the Parking Bureau instituted a policy where getting a reduction almost always means getting the fine cut in half (although usually rounded up), so for example a $115 ticket would be reduced to $60. Of course, every "fair" policy has its consequences: Now even the person with the stellar excuse will still walk out with a hefty blow to the wallet. Isn't it funny how unfair being fair can be? Here too, if you know that half just won't do it for you – fight in person. After all, you never know; maybe you'll find that one judge who isn't scared to fight City Hall.

## 25. How to Delay Paying a Ticket

This section ought to be subtitled "how to work the system." If you're dead guilty but you don't have the cash to cough up right now and you want to avoid the pecuniary pain for as long as possible, you can do it in the following way:

First, never fight the ticket through the Internet, through certified mail or going to a live hearing. Of the three, the Internet is the slowest (if you fight through certified mail, by law you're guaranteed a quick response) and yet the slowest of this bunch – fighting via the Web – is still quick. Too quick.

What you want to do is to write out your defense on old-fashioned paper and send it in by regular mail. Having mailed in your defense, you're officially in the system – so they can't give you late fees. But with a usual backlog of at least four months of tickets in the Parking Bureau, this alone will delay your payment by a third of a year.

Next, you want to make sure

> Ninety eight percent of the adults in this country are decent, hardworking, honest Americans. It's the other lousy two percent that get all the publicity. But then, we elected them.
>
> – Lily Tomlin

that your defense requires you to take photos. This part is a bit of a gamble (and if you think you have a real shot at winning by showing photos, then send them of course), but generally, if your defense needs pictures, and you haven't included them, you'll get a thirty day adjournment. Armed with this adjournment, when you send in your defense again, *with* the photos, do it by regular mail (of course), and after a solid three weeks have gone by, your ticket will once again go to the bottom of the new mail pile – buying yourself yet another few months of delay. All told, this tactic can have you paying for a February ticket in December. By which time, the vagaries of holiday mail will mean your check will take twice as long to get there and be cashed.

Voilà.

# 26. Things Always Worth Doing & Things Never Worth Doing

Too many people make the worst kind of mistake when fighting tickets: The kind that is easily avoidable. This section is a run-down of some of the most problematic, and sometimes obvious, mistakes that people make. Do yourself a favor and join the ranks of people who *don't* make them.

## You Should Always:

(1) Defend your ticket. If you don't play you can't win. Every year millions of people pay for tickets that are defective simply by not taking the trouble to send in the most cursory defense. If nothing else, send back a letter with the summons number and a note saying "please check for defects."

(2) Spell check. We won't hold it against you legally, but the more grammatically correct your defense is, the easier it is to read. Don't make judges sweat in order to figure out what you're saying.

(3) Be legible. Typewritten or neatly handwritten de-

fenses are a joy to read. Hastily scribbled and illegible cursive script, written on the back of the ticket in ever-decreasing size as you run out of space, is a nightmare. And it won't make you any friends.

(4) Use a separate page. You're better off not writing your defense on the back of the ticket at all. Invest in a whole brand new sheet of paper. In fact, you're generally better off not sending in your ticket at all – just send in the violation number.

(5) Include an actual defense. Even if it's just the words "please check for defects." Don't just send in the ticket or a photograph without any explanation whatsoever.

(6) Tell us a story. The more we identify with you and understand what happened, the greater the likelihood that we'll believe your version of the events and want to at least reduce the fine. Don't just say "I didn't do it."

(7) If you have a witness, come down in person. And bring him. A live witness can be questioned and believed. One that exists only in a letter could be a figment of your imagination. And no, the judge will not call to confirm. The only possible exception to this would be if you send in a notarized affidavit by your witness with your defense. But live is still ever so much better.

(8) Come down in person if your explanation is complicated. If you tell your friends your excuse and they have to ask you a bunch of questions until they understand you, don't assume that the judge will get it without having the same opportunity to question you. Go to a live hearing and let him fire away. The alternative is having the judge confused and unpersuaded.

(9) Write in "please check for legibility." The judges are supposed to do this anyway, but by bringing to their attention that it matters to you, you'll be more likely to

benefit from any doubts in borderline cases. The reason is that the judge will now have to consider not just whether *he* thinks it's legible, but whether the Appellate Panel will agree with him when you appeal.

(10) Include all paperwork. If you're relying on a previous dismissal – send in a copy of it. If you're relying on your employee's testimony – send in his affidavit. If the fire department sent you a letter saying that the hydrant is permanently broken – show us the letter. You get the point.

(11) If pictures are necessary for your defense, send in photos of the entire street, corner to corner.

(12) Keep a copy of whatever you're sending in. You never know what could get lost.

(13) Appeal. Even if you have only a small shot of winning (see the section on Appeals).

(14) Realize that the whole city is a tow-away zone. Even when the signs *don't* warn you. But take heart: If you succeed in beating your parking ticket, you'll get the towing charge dismissed too.

> Your Honor:
>    I am outraged at this ticket. As a law-abiding citizen I pay the taxes that support your salary and I demand that you cancel this ticket. This ticket violates public policy! If you refuse to cancel this ticket, you leave me no alternative but to schedule a hearing along with our attorney.

**You Should Never:**

(1) Include your phone number in your mailed-in or web-based defense. There's no point – we won't call. There isn't even a phone available to us for such purposes.

(2) Send or bring in your copy of the ticket. You're much better off forcing the judge to look at only the official ticket (the one on the judge's screen). There are plenty of times where something on the official ticket is only

borderline legible (due to bad scanning, for example), and if the judge is looking only at that ticket he'll consider it defective. If, however, he sees the hard copy you brought in, he's reading that official ticket with far less scrutiny. After all, he already *knows* what the expiration date is on your registration – he's not trying to figure it out from the official ticket.

The only exception to this rule is where the cop did not check off *any* violation on your ticket. In that case, you should win because of a technical defect. And you want to show the judge that the cop left the ticket blank, because cops (unfortunately) cheat too and sometimes will "correct" their official tickets after they've given you your copy, and before they're scanned into the system. (3) Make your case so complicated that no one can understand it – even when you're available to be questioned. Keeping it simple is more effective. Truly.

(4) Try to snow over the judge by being too vague or using the passive voice too much. It generally won't work.

(5) Use web-based services that will fight your ticket for you. They hurt your credibility, because they use canned language. As one judge put it: "They just fill in the blanks, throwing everything in, making things up. Who can believe them?"

(6) Send in a coffee-stained response. If you can't read it easily, we can't read it at all.

(7) Cry, curse, threaten the judge, call the judge names, be insulting, use profanity or make racist comments. It's shocking how many people lose control over their emotions. Don't be one of them.

(8) Assume anything. Many people have misconceptions about what the law is. Hopefully, by reading this

book you won't be one of them. Some common misconceptions: believing that double parking is okay if you leave someone in the car; thinking that they can't tow you from that spot (the whole city is a tow-away zone); and assuming that just because you have a good excuse you'll get off. This can be said another way: Don't believe everything your friends tell you about parking tickets. Chances are they're wrong. And never trust a cop's word either. They aren't the judges, they're often wrong – and it's not *their* greenbacks on the line.

(9) Write in that you have witnesses. A witness is great – if you bring them in to a live hearing. And it's at least sometimes effective if you get them to write a letter on your behalf (or better yet, a notarized affidavit) testifying to their version. But just telling us that someone else saw what happened won't help. And yes, that's true even if you've provided us with their e-mail or phone number. Don't even bother.

(10) Commit fraud. Examples of fraud are abundant, from altering the license plate number on the ticket to telling unusual lies on every single summons you receive. Plan on forging meter receipts? Or altering your registration sticker? Take five – it's all been done before. In fact, I'd bet dollars to doughnuts that most of us can't even come up with an original fraud that'll actually work.

Seriously, though, if you get caught committing fraud, not only will you have to pay for the ticket (including previous tickets you may have already gotten away with), you'll also get an extra $60 fine on top of your original fine and *then* they'll triple the whole shebang. So if you get caught on five tickets that were each originally $115 – they'll slap you with a fine of $525 for each ticket: $2,625. Ouch!

(11) Bother to ask for the Parking Bureau to send you "any other tickets I might have." They won't and you'll end up forgetting to check for them yourself – thereby opening the way to finding yourself with default judgments (see Chapter 27) for tickets you didn't ever pay.

## 27. Tickets in Default Judgment

If you are anything like the rest of us, chances are that you didn't rush out to pay your ticket the very second that you got it. And even if you've decided to defend the ticket (as you always should), it's all too easy to let some time pass before actually getting around to doing it.

If you're lucky and you live in New York State, the Parking Bureau will send you notices reminding you to either pay up or defend yourself. But if you've managed to ignore all of these reminders, or you live outside of New York State, where you get only one notice, and ninety days go by without your response, your silence will be considered an admission of guilt – and your ticket will enter what's known as a "default judgment."

Default judgment for a parking ticket means that if you want to extricate yourself from the fines and penalties you not only need a good reason to get out of the ticket, you need a reason why the judge should even *listen* to your reason, considering the amount of time that has passed. You need, in other words, to prove that you committed what's known as "excusable neglect."

The way it works is this: Once your ticket has been

entered into judgment, in order for the judge to hear you out, the ticket first has to be taken *out* of judgment. To do that, you have to make what's known as a "motion to vacate" the judgment.

There are certain rules when it comes to motions to vacate. The most important is that you need to show two things in order to win. First, you need to explain why you failed to respond to the ticket and all the subsequent notices. Second, you need to show that you have a "substantial defense" – that is, one that has merit to it – for the ticket itself [The Commissioner's Rules, Section 39–10(i)].

> **When you go into court you are putting your fate into the hands of twelve people who weren't smart enough to get out of jury duty.**
>
> **– Norm Crosby**

Other rules are more banal but still need to be followed. For example, all motions to vacate must be in writing (there are forms to help you). And that written motion must be signed only by the person whose judgment it is or by their live-in spouse. What that means in practice is that if you want your ticket to be fought at a live hearing, you can't send down your parent or boyfriend or sister, even if you've given them a letter authorizing them to do it for you – you have to go down there yourself. On the other hand, if you're mailing in your defense then just mail in the motion to vacate too. Incidentally, if it's a corporation that got the judgment, then any authorized officer or employee is sufficient.

But as a whole, what trips people up most often is the first rule – giving the reason why they didn't respond on time to begin with. The trouble is that you need to come up with a reason that is *good*.

Examples of good reasons for not having responded

for months are scarce, but here are a few right off the bat:

(1) You were hospitalized. No judge is going to penalize you for being too sick to answer. The caveat? No judge is going to take you on your word alone, either. To win with this one (and this is true for most excuses) make sure to bring in documentation. For example, copies of your hospital bill or records.

(2) You were out of the country. Bring in your passport and/or any other proof that you can find. The same logic as hospitalization applies. On the other hand, if you lent your car to someone while you were out of the country and *they* got the ticket, your being out of the country won't help you.

(3) You were thrown out of the house by your evil step-mother. This one I actually got once and the kid made such a convincing case (including details of mail being intercepted) that I granted his motion. Still, it's a harder one to win, for obvious reasons.

The trick to remember with good excuses is that the reason that they're good is that there was nothing you could have done to prevent them from happening. If, on the other hand, there was something you could have or should have done, the excuse is, shall we say, less than great.

Take, for example, the classic excuse that we hear so often: The notice was sent to the wrong address. This sounds like a great excuse in theory, and it's often the honest-to-God truth, but it has one built-in problem that most people tend to forget: You have a legal duty to notify the DMV of your new address within ten days. Which means that you probably won't get too much sympathy from the Parking Bureau.

Other problems with this excuse are that a judge is likely to ask why you didn't tell the post office about your new address, and how you suddenly found out about the ticket now. All in all, not one of the better reasons to try to pin "excusable neglect" on. And, incidentally, it's the address that your vehicle is registered to that counts – not the one printed on your driver's license.

Other examples of excuses that you should avoid are the following "classic" bad excuses: Having had no money earlier; having been too busy to deal with the ticket; having lent someone the car and therefore you didn't know about the ticket; having phoned the Parking Bureau and "someone told me not to worry"; and having felt that the ticket was unfair to begin with.

What all of these excuses have in common is that no one doubts that they might be true (except possibly the phone call to PVB); the problem is that none of them are compelling enough to vacate a judgment.

For example, not having money, or being too busy, are almost never good reasons, in the eyes of the law, for ignoring a legal duty (in this case, to respond to the ticket). There are just too many people who are too poor or too busy. Ditto for feeling that the ticket wasn't fair to begin with. How many people feel that a parking ticket is *ever* fair?

> Judge:
> Because I am no working and I not living at this address. It must be the Mailing office. That not my folt and those ticked not call for because I was not barking the violations.

In fact, the only reason, of the ones listed above, that ought to be a good one is lending your car to someone. And in a case like that, the Parking Bureau essentially feels that you should either collect the money from *them* or learn your lesson for being too trusting. This, by the way, applies especially to parents of teenagers. The judge will probably sympathize with you – but you heard it here first: Find a better excuse.

But let's say that you have found a better excuse, and you do have a reasonable cause for not having responded – i.e. "excusable neglect" is taken care of. Now you have to remember the second rule: You need a meritorious defense to the ticket – the violation – itself.

Since this is what the bulk of this book is about, there's no need for me to repeat every type of defense here. The reason to stress this rule here at all is this: You must bring in or send in your defense to the ticket itself *at the same time* as you make the motion to vacate. This means that you must have already taken all of your photographs, and if you're bringing in witnesses, they must be there with you. It's no good to take care of the motion now, and figure that you'll send in the "real" defense later.

In addition, when it comes to tickets in judgment, it's generally a good idea to bring your original ticket(s) with you. Right or wrong, there are judges who will deny your motion to vacate for five tickets if you only show them four of the tickets. Don't give them this opportunity. Take your tickets with you, or send them in (this is obviously an exception to my usual advice to never bring in the original summons). This will also help you if there is an obvious technical defect, such as a missing item on the face of the ticket.

With motions to vacate, the technical defects are a bit different than usual (there are some technical defects that won't be as effective), but if something is obviously wrong with the summons, your best bet is if the judge sees it immediately.

Finally, there are a few more points to know:

(1) You have a maximum of one year to make a motion to vacate. Don't go counting on a judge buying into an "extraordinary circumstance" defense to bend this time limit.

(2) If you're claiming that you already sent in your defense earlier and the PVB lost it, you should know that sending tickets in by certified mail will *compel* the Parking Bureau, by law, to respond within forty-five days. So if you can show your receipt, and there is no response on record, your ticket will be dismissed [see VTL section 237(8)].

(3) Motions to vacate are almost never adjourned, so if you need to bring documents and you forgot to, turn around and go back and get them. The judge probably won't hear your motion if you're not ready.

(4) There is no point in pleading guilty to the ticket but making a motion to vacate to get off of the penalties for being late. In practice, this won't work. What happens is that the judge *must* rule on your motion to vacate first. And part of what you need to win that motion is the fact that you have a meritorious defense to the underlying violation. Even a "hanging by a thread" defense is better here than none at all. Even one that says simply "there are technical defects" could do the trick.

If you actually have a good reason for not responding on time, but don't have a winning defense for your violation, then the judge will grant your motion to vacate and then look at the ticket itself. Then – and only then – will the judge be able to give you a verdict of "guilty" on the violation but then decide to reduce or eliminate the late penalties for you (due to your "excusable neglect").

None of this is obvious, by any means. And in some ways, it doesn't even make sense. But sometimes, as Dickens might say, "the law is an ass." And the only way to deal with it is to arm yourself with knowledge.

To sum up, if you have a ticket in default, don't despair. You *can* beat it. Just remember the advice above and fight it the right way. With any luck, your motion to vacate will be granted and your ticket itself will be dismissed.

**Recap: The Least You Need to Know:**

- Not responding within ninety days is considered an admission of guilt.
- To get a default judgment lifted, you need to make a motion to vacate.
- The motion must show "excusable neglect" for not responding, and a "meritorious defense" to the violation itself.
- The motion must be granted first; only then will the underlying defense be considered.
- You must bring or send in all of your proofs for the underlying defense at the same time as you make the motion to vacate.
- Don't bother with excuses such as you were too busy or had no money.
- If you lend your car to someone who then screws up, PVB will not let you off the hook.

## 28. Appeals – When to Do Them and How they Work

The appeals process is probably the most under-utilized resource that ticket-fighters have. As it is, around eighty percent of tickets are just paid, without a fight. But of the twenty percent that are defended, only a tiny fraction of those people who are found guilty bother to take it "all the way." If nothing else, I hope that this section convinces you to be one of those few, those happy few.

### How to Win an Appeal

After you get your guilty verdict (and after you stop cussing out the Judge in your head) you need to pay the ticket and immediately file for an appeal. But first you need to know what it is that the Appeals Board is going to be looking at when it scans your file. What are the standards and how can you use them to win your appeal?

Officially, the rule is that the Appeals Board will reverse a decision only if the trial decision was arbitrary, capricious or involved some mistake of law or mistake of fact. What that means in practice is not always obvious or even consistent.

First, the bad news: There are definitely times when the Appeals Board upholds decisions that have glaring errors in them. How do I know this? Simple; I still recall vividly the time I was talking to a group of senior judges and one of them mentioned, in passing, a case that she thought should have been reversed. Her comment? "I don't know how PVB gets away with some of those decisions."

And then there was the case of the senior judge who always found people guilty of double parking – even when the law allowed it. And her comment to me, when defending her error, was this gem: "Well, I've never been reversed on appeal."

These examples don't even include all the times when a trial judge makes a bad judgment call that *doesn't* quite rise to a level of a "reversible error of law or fact." Like the judge that knocked down a defense to a "no standing/trucks loading" ticket sent in by a commercial firm which claimed that they were there for a long time because they needed to fix an elevator. Their defense was that they were on an "emergency service call" because people were stuck in an elevator. The judge's attitude? That being stuck wasn't a "real" emergency. "Would you consider being stuck in a train an emergency?" she asked "I wouldn't." And this, *after* the events of 9/11…

So if the appeal process is so unfair, should you still bother?

Absolutely.

Because you really can win.

I once had a private conversation with one judge who

sat regularly on the Appeals Board, who mentioned that they throw out "hundreds" of decisions simply because the (handwritten) decisions were not legible.

And another judge told me an astonishing little trick of the trade: Appeals that ask for a review of the tape of their live hearing are often successful for the all-too-stupid reason that the PVB sometimes loses the tape!

In addition, there are plenty of judges who are not careful about the way they word their verdicts, whether in a live hearing or a mailed-in one. So, for instance, when it comes to a respondent who wrote in a general denial (i.e. "I never parked there"), it's often all too tempting for the trial judge to simply write "the respondent's claim fails to persuade me that the officer/ticket was incorrect" or some such statement. By including the words "officer" or "ticket" the judge has inadvertently told the absolute truth – that the ticket is more believable. But, as one Appeals judge said to me, "if the judge says that he didn't believe you because the officer said the opposite, it will get reversed – otherwise, why bother even having a judge?" The idea here is that when a judge listens to your testimony (or reads it) he is really presiding over a mini-trial. First came the officer's testimony (the ticket) and now comes yours. The judge doesn't have to think your testimony is credible – he can say that he's not persuaded by it. But if the only *reason* that he's unpersuaded is because the officer/ticket says the opposite – it sounds very much like the judge just didn't listen to your testimony at all. Which is a definite no-no. So, this is a subtle point, but can still lead an appeals board to say that the judge screwed up.

In a similar vein, if the decision is worded in such a way that it seems that the only reason the judge found against you was that he or she checked the DMV or DOT records (which indicated that you were lying), you have a good shot of winning your appeal. Why? Because when you're defending your ticket the burden of proof is on the officer (that is, the ticket), not on you. So if you testify to something that is the opposite of what the DMV or DOT records show, the judge has to technically decide, up front, whether your testimony was credible. Only then can he state that your defense was not persuasive. By writing that he was relying on the records alone, he is essentially saying that he side-stepped his responsibility to weigh *all* your evidence.

These are subtle differences that we're talking about. But in those subtle gaps lie the hope of a dismissed ticket.

Furthermore, there are some decisions which don't say much about anything at all. They say, frankly, too little. These are tickets worth appealing, because if the Appeals Board can't follow the trial judge's analysis (because the decision is too general, for example), there's a good chance that the appeal will be successful on that basis alone.

Also, there are plenty of decisions which don't seem to relate to the case that you presented. The trial judge is supposed to address *all* the defenses that you brought up. If the judge forgot to do that – you have a good argument on appeal. I should point out that this is *not* a reason for you to make your original defense full of gobbledygook, or so vague and complicated that the trial judge is likely to

> I was married by a judge. I should have asked for a jury.
>
> – Groucho Marx

forget something. If you do, you're more likely just to anger the Appeals Board than anything else.

So what *should* you do on your original defense? You should read the pertinent sections of this book and make sure that you include the law in your defense. If you were legally in the right – tell them! That way, if you get a guilty verdict you can point out that the trial judge made a "reversible error of law." Similarly, make your facts iron-clad obvious – include documentation. Get affidavits from witnesses. Bring in photographs. That way, if the trial judge says that he doesn't believe you that there was such a sign there, you have the incontestable proof that he made a "reversible error of fact."

And, by the way, don't leave anything out of your original defense, hoping to "save it" for the appeal. Although technically the Appeals Board has the power to look at new evidence, in practice they almost never do. They will, however, try to review your original defense (particularly if it was sent in by mail). So throw in every defense that can work for you. Review this book; scour it for excuses that apply. Avoid the ones that won't get you out of the batter's box. Don't be shy about telling the trial judge the whole story of how you got that ticket. Remember, your chances for a successful appeal start at the trial stage.

And when you make your appeal, avoid calling the trial judge that found you guilty an idiot. Say that he or she made a mistake; they misunderstood the law as it applied to you, or they got one of the facts wrong. In short, make it easy for the judges sitting on the Appeals Board to say "oops, I guess the trial judge goofed on this one."

And definitely take the time to make the appeal. The journey to a successful defense often finally concludes only when you reach the Appeals Board.

### Recap: The Least You Need to Know:

- It's almost always worth appealing.
- If your verdict was handwritten, check for legibility.
- Decisions are reversed because of mistakes of law, mistakes of fact or because they were arbitrary.
- The judge must have answered *all* your defenses.
- The wording of the verdict may give you a good chance to win, even though they had you "dead to rights."

# Index

## About the Author

Haskell Nussbaum is an attorney and a freelance writer who worked as a parking ticket judge in New York City. While there, he adjudicated thousands of tickets and collected stories and insights from many judges, to make *Beat That Parking Ticket, A Complete Guide for New York City* the most comprehensive behind-the-scenes guide to fighting parking tickets. He can be reached at Nussbaum@beatthatparkingticket.com.

# Call for Stories

If you have an interesting or crazy story involving a parking ticket, send it to us! All submissions will be reviewed for possible inclusion in a later edition of this book or a related book. Drop us a line at stories@gavelpress.com. For more information, visit us at *www.BeatThatParkingTicket.com*